CAMBRIDGE
THE HIDDEN HISTORY

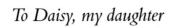

To Daisy, my daughter

CAMBRIDGE

THE HIDDEN HISTORY

ALISON TAYLOR

TEMPUS

First published 1999
First paperback edition 2001
Reprinted 2004

Tempus Publishing Ltd
The Mill, Brimscombe Port
Stroud, Gloucestershire GL5 2QG
www.tempus-publishing.com

British Library Cataloguing in Publication Data.
A catalogue record for this book is available from the British Library.

ISBN 0 7524 1914 5

Typesetting and origination by Tempus Publishing.
Printed and bound in Great Britain.

Contents

List of illustrations

Colour plates

The front cover shows excavations by Cambridge Archeological Unit of the Provost's Lodge outside Kings College

Acknowledgements

This volume has been based on the work of a great number of scholars and archaeologists, past and present. One of my greatest debts is to the Cambridge Antiquarian Society itself, which for more than a century has published the results of these people's observations and research. I have drawn heavily on their publications for information and illustrations, and am very grateful for both. This Society is also the owner of the early nineteenth century drawings of Richard Relhan, which are deposited in the University Library. Another invaluable resource for both data and illustration is the Cambridgeshire Collection, part of Cambridgeshire's library service. Chris Jakes and the other staff of this collection have been enormously helpful in loaning and copying material, and many photographs derive from their store. Two archaeological organisations, the Cambridge Archaeology Unit and the County's Archaeological Field Unit have loaned innumerable site reports and kept me up to date with the latest finds. For additional information on historic buildings I am grateful to Chris Godfrey of the County's Conservation Section, for details on modern Cambridge to officers of Cambridge City Council, and for further archaeological data to the County's Sites and Monuments Record. Volumes of the Victoria County History, as noted in the bibliography, are invaluable, particularly for medieval historical records, and I am especially grateful to Andrew Wareham of VCH for data on Cherry Hinton in advance of publication.

Many individuals have helped with advice and detailed information. These include Tim Reynolds on Palaeolithic finds, Tony Baggs on the Civil War, Tom Doig on background to the Folk Museum, Mike Petty on developments in Cambridge in the nineteenth and twentieth centuries, and Derek Stubbing on the history of Chesterton. Peter Bryant has also been exceptionally kind in letting me see work he has done on the historical geography and later history of the town, and Honor Ridout's research on Sturbridge Fair was invaluable. Illustrations are an important part of a work of this kind and, apart from the institutions noted above, I have been helped with photographs taken by Gwil Owen of Cambridge University Museum of Archaeology and Anthropology, and with loans by Belinda Parham and Geoffrey Robinson. Thanks also go to Sarah Wroot, who drew the maps for the distribution of finds and for Anglo-Saxon Cambridge.

Introduction

Cambridge today is a city of nearly 110,000 people living in an area covering just over 4000 hectares, within which lie visible evidence for an extraordinary past and hidden clues for a long history of great complexity. This book will look at the whole of that history, from the flint tools of prehistory to college buildings of international renown, but the emphasis will be on the roots and developing life of a country town. Within the overall story there are plots that merit whole volumes of their own: Iron Age forts, a Roman town, one of England's richest Anglo-Saxon cemeteries, a medieval castle, a great European fair, and of course its university, are a few examples. Of these, the university and its colleges are well covered in many publications but, although there has been research on other aspects of the town, little of this has been published since the pioneering days of the late nineteenth and early twentieth centuries, and so this book is weighted towards them.

Geography and geology have affected development here in various ways, often through the negative impact of adverse factors. The town lies within the bend of a broad, sluggish river whose shifting course, wide flood-plain and multiple channels limited normal development yet brought wealth to its doorstep. The peculiar difficulties of this river mostly worked to Cambridge's advantage; upstream it was only navigable for the shallowest punts, and downstream the muddy alluvium along its banks restricted use of ferries and made bridge building impossible until 1890. The coincidence of being both the lowest bridging point and highest site for unloading cargo made the area around the Great (now Magdalene) Bridge a natural cross-road and trading centre. The river too could act as either barrier or gateway. It made a natural tribal division, effective at certain points in Iron Age and Anglo-Saxon times, but because east-west routes that skirted the Fens had to pass through this bridging point it opened East Anglia to the midlands and other parts of Britain. Most crucially of all it gave access to Europe. Trade therefore flourished and new ideas came in quickly, but vulnerability to attack was a less enviable result.

Within the town there were also natural forces that had positive and negative effects. In very broad terms Cambridge is a shallow hollow with outcrops of chalk and clay forming higher land at the sides, a band of alluvium following the river at the bottom, and ridges of gravel interrupted by old and current watercourses over most of the rest (**8**). The chalk outcrops were used for fortifications, notably on Castle Hill and War Ditches, the alluvium was generally uninhabitable except for seasonal prehistoric camp sites, and gravel soils were only habitable in early periods where they were a little more than 10 metres above sea level. Higher ground within the historic centre was used for roads and settlements, as can be seen from the routes of the two main streets through the town and the sites chosen for churches in the Saxon period (**23**). Slightly lower gravels were built up as a by-product of urban rubbish deposits during the middle ages. To most observers the lower town of Cambridge south and east of the river is now basically flat, and the upper town to the north-west barely seems a hill to those from outside Cambridgeshire.

There are hints even in Bronze Age times that the Cambridge area was starting to be seen as a regional centre, and by the Late Iron Age it is evident that the upper town in particular was a seat of power and commerce and that settlement around it was dense and widespread. These characteristics were further developed in the Roman upper town, but when we first get a picture of the Anglo-Saxon town there has been a change which was to be permanent. Defence and administration were by then based on the hill-top, within the old Roman walls, but the market place, docks and most of the settlement were in the *lower* town, bounded by a water-filled ditch that follows a natural depression.

Around Cambridge at all periods there was a highly productive rural landscape, one of the most densely settled in Britain in the middle ages. The Fens that came within five miles of Cambridge to the north were the most unusual part of this landscape, abundant in wild products such as wild fowl, fish, turves and sedge for strewing on floors, all much valued by an urban population and with a ready export market. The Fen edges where periodic flooding occurred were also invaluable for fattening cattle for townsmen with inadequate grazing, and were renowned for their production of butter and cheese. Such productivity made the Fens an important part of Cambridge's hinterland from at least Roman times, and continued even after the environment had been changed by drainage in the seventeenth century. Cambridge was surrounded on its other sides by more traditional agricultural areas. Gravel soils along the Cam, Rhee and Granta valleys were used for mixed farming from Neolithic times and, wherever there were fords in this hospitable countryside, later groups of farmsteads were liable to grow into villages or even small towns. Higher clay plateaux were less hospitable but when there was enough labour to farm the heavy land intensively they proved fertile. Medieval villages for example clustered there most thickly of all, though in later years the populations fell as the proportion of pasture to arable increased. The broad band of chalk across southern Cambridgeshire had quite different values. Much of it could not be settled for lack of water and yet its dry open character, part of a range that stretched from south-western England to East Anglia, made it a natural highway. Its open heaths were also good sheep country, their flocks supporting several Roman villas and giving additional incomes to villagers in adjoining parishes right up to Enclosure in the mid nineteenth century.

Varied products from these regions boosted Cambridge as a market centre, though it was its national and European links via the Cam and the Wash that differentiated it from most country towns. The life of this hinterland was entwined with Cambridge in other ways too, for landowners down to quite humble levels had property in both town and country. Villagers commonly migrated to the town, giving families ties in both, and the lifestyles of those who relied on labouring in the fields and use of common rights varied little from their neighbours in the countryside.

Certain patterns are apparent throughout history and prehistory: Cambridge as a local centre but with access to a wider world; possessing good transport systems but not bothered by a situation actually on a national highway; regionally important for defence and administration but usually not in a dangerous frontier zone. Other themes that recur are the rural nature of life within the town, down to the cows that came in for milking in the twentieth century and the sheep and cattle still grazing on the greens, commons and Backs, and also the notable absence of an industrial base beyond the supply of local needs. Instead, the interlinked worlds of religion, ritual, education and intellectual thought thrived, and in the middle ages become a distinctive lifestyle, dominated by the communities of monastic houses and colleges. Meanwhile other circles developed in their own ways, also working as village-like communities within the urban landscape.

From late Saxon times Cambridge was the county town for an area that roughly covered the present city and South Cambridgeshire. Chesterton, Cherry Hinton and Trumpington were brought within the town boundaries in 1912 and 1935, and in 1951 Cambridge was legally made a city. It has been the centre for an expanded county from 1974, and offices for Cambridgeshire and South Cambridgeshire authorities, as well as those for Cambridge itself and many central government services, are now situated in the town. Its life is no longer much affected by the boundaries and constraints of earlier years but, as the following chapters show, there is no escape from a history of this kind.

1 Before a town was built: Cambridge in prehistory

The earliest traces of human habitation, those of the Palaeolithic period, have to be sought well below modern ground levels, in layers of gravel deposited before the last Ice Age. Cambridge's site in the Cam valley is one of the few areas in Britain where some of these layers and the flint tools and animal bones they contain escaped the scouring effects of later glaciations, lying undisturbed below up to 15 metres of gravel. Probably the oldest finds are those from sites near the Huntingdon Road west of Cambridge, where hand-axes and flake scrapers of Acheulian type, dating between 360-130,000 BC, were found in a quarry (**1**). Several hundred flint tools, some of them lying undisturbed since they were used, were collected here. Pollen from a site belonging to the next warm phase, the Ipswichian (130-105,000 BC), at Histon Road shows how the climate changed at that time from a fairly warm spell that allowed mixed oak forests to develop, to a cooler period dominated by coniferous forests. Remains of molluscs, indicating warm temperatures, were also found here. Quarries at Barnwell produced evidence for conditions in the last Ice Age, (the Devensian, between 105-12,000 BC). Here there was an Arctic flora and cold climate snails, insects and mammals. An elephant rib-bone, worked by humans, was an exceptional find from this site. From other sites on Newmarket and Milton Roads, where gravel quarries were dug near the river on the outskirts of Cambridge in the late nineteenth century, flint hand-axes and bones of elephant, rhinoceros and hippopotamus were found by workmen and are now in the Sedgwick Museum.

The tools of later hunter-gathering societies, those of the Mesolithic period (roughly 7,500-3,000 BC), lie close to modern ground surfaces but are rarely reported because, unlike the impressive hand-axes of Palaeolithic times, they are generally small and insignificant enough to escape detection during normal soil disturbance. One interesting collection was made at Ditton Meadows, now in the flood-plain of the Cam, on land ideal for temporary settlements when sea-levels were lower than they are today. Tools found here included scrapers, borers and microliths, as well as waste flakes and the flint-cores from which the small tools of the period had been made, evidence that people stayed here long enough to need fresh equipment.

By Neolithic times (about 3,000-2000 BC), cultural changes in Britain included the introduction of farming, use of pottery, and a range of well-crafted stone tools. It was now possible for people to build houses and settle in one area, but it is often forgotten what a good living could still be made from mixing a little agriculture with use of the wild resources of the forests, fens and river. It is therefore not surprising that only one site with

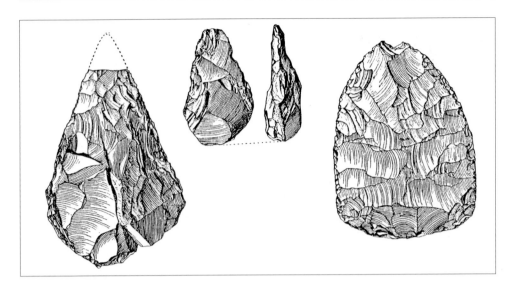

1   Palaeolithic tools found near Huntingdon Road. Scale 1:2

any sort of *permanent* settlement has been recognised so far, found in anti-tank traps being dug to prevent any German advance on Cambridge from the east during World War II. In true Cambridge tradition there was an archaeologist on hand to make a record of a pit cut into chalk, presumably made for storage and containing late Neolithic decorated pottery, bones of a sheep and a small ox, and numerous flakes left from flint working. A similar pit was found on the opposite side of Hills Road, and finds made by recent field-walking in the area show that a settlement existed here for some time. Elsewhere in Cambridge water-levels were still lower than in later years but in areas near the Cam only pockets of land would have been attractive for farming settlements, although there is plenty of evidence they were often chosen for temporary camps by seasonal visitors. Gravel diggings at Ditton Meadows and recent investigations for college developments near the Cam, such as Jesus College library and Trinity's student accommodation on Burrell's Walk, have revealed scatters of waste flints, broken tools and pot-boilers left after heating water with hot stones, typical of camps that might be used for a few weeks each year. Also, Neolithic axes are quite a common find in Cambridge gardens. These fine tools had many uses, but felling trees is the most obvious, and their concentration here, as around the fen-edge north of Cambridge, suggests that people whose homes were elsewhere jouneyed into the forests for timber, hunting and shooting, and to gather food-stuffs and wild resources.

As populations grew during the succeeding Bronze Age the human impact on the environment becomes more evident, and there are hints that by the Late Bronze Age the Cambridge area was beginning to act as a local power base. The fort at War Ditches, for example, may well have originated at this time, for there were sherds of Bronze Age pottery in its ditch, and near the fort there were at least two Bronze Age burial mounds. More significantly, there were two exceptionally large hoards of used bronze tools and scrap buried in pits in Chesterton, near to the river in the north of Cambridge. One hoard consisted of twenty one axes, a spear, gouge, ring and freshly smelted metal (**2**). The tools

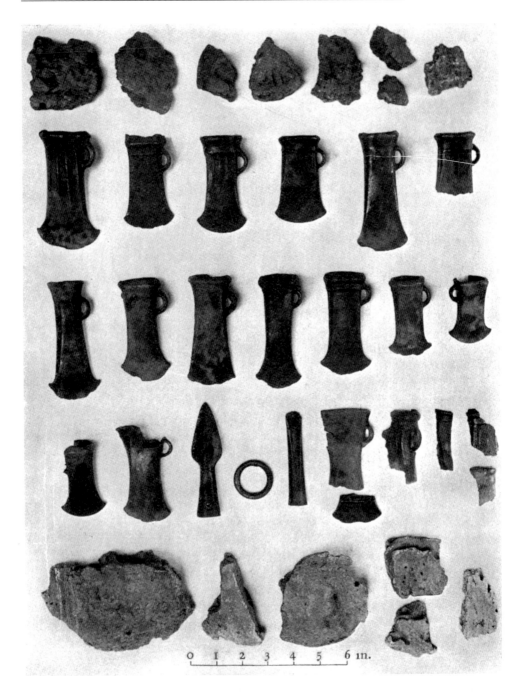

2   *A hoard of Bronze Age tools and smelted metal from Chesterton*

were all worn or damaged, and some had been deliberately flattened. The second hoard, found in a sack that had been left in a small pit, was larger, including twenty axes, two spears, parts of a sword and a rapier, three gouges, a chisel, awl, two rings, other fragments, and a large amount of rough metal. Together these tools and weapons provide a picture of the normal equipment available at this time. They had clearly been collected and stored ready for melting down and re-working into whatever was needed next. Such collections are often said to be the forgotten hoards of travelling smiths, but they seem to occur too frequently and include too much random material for this to be likely. More probably, the stock was held at a tribal centre or other accessible but secure point, to be dipped into as and when new items were required. A mould for making the sorts of axe found in the hoards was discovered in New Street in central Cambridge, a further indication that tools were being manufactured here.

Burial sites of the Early and Middle Bronze Age cluster in this region, both in the river valley and on the southern chalk ridge. None survive as upstanding mounds, but a few of the burials that lay within them have been excavated. At Cherry Hinton, infilled quarry ditches that surrounded the mounds have been recognised from the air, and recent excavations in one of these has revealed cremated remains from the centre and Bronze Age pottery and waste flints from the surrounding ditch. Ditches of two similar mounds were noticed during quarrying near War Ditches. Close to the river on Midsummer Common a group of complete early Bronze Age pots must have been the grave goods that accompanied similar barrow burials, and a beaker excavated nearby, under Elizabeth Way, was presumably yet another.

Mixed agriculture and more settled occupation sites are generally a feature of this period, but traces of these are hard to find in the disturbed soils around Cambridge. Stray finds that are reported, (metal axes, rapiers dredged from the river, flint arrow heads and other flint implements) indicate that much of the landscape was still exploited for its wild resources, as in the Neolithic. A yew bow from Cambridge, preserved in peat and dated by radiocarbon to approximately 1730 BC, would also fit with this use of the landscape.

It was during the Iron Age (from about 700 BC) that farming settlements were finally established widely in the Cam valley. Their ditched fields, enclosed farmsteads, storage pits and abundant rubbish are easily detected in comparison with the ephemeral traces of earlier cultures, and it is clear that the population was rising fast now that food was more consistently available. At the same time, competition for land, and the ease with which a sedentary population could be controlled by armed powers increased a tendency, already visible during the Bronze Age, for society to split into class-based structures based on military power. Cambridge was sited on a crucial bridging point at the boundary of powerful territorial units, and the archaeological remains of its humble farmers and craftsmen are dwarfed by forts, other defended centres and the rich burials of their rulers. The major tribes whose disputed territorial boundaries were in the Cambridge region are known by name in Late Iron Age times, because their interaction with Rome meant they at last entered the written record. Their territories can be roughly plotted because they now used coins which bore the names of rulers. They were principally the Trinovantes from around Colchester, and the Catuvellauni, based in Verulamium, with the Iceni of Norfolk impacting from the north.

3   *An early excavation of War Ditches*

Wandlebury hill fort, three miles south-east of Cambridge, commanded the Icknield Way route and approaches to Cambridge from that direction. There were also circular fortifications at Arbury Camp to the north, and War Ditches in Cherry Hinton to the east. Arbury Camp, about 100 metres in diameter and now flattened by ploughing, was trenched in 1990, showing that there had been a massive timber gateway and a deep waterlogged ditch still containing many fragments of leather. Deep ploughing of the interior meant that no signs of occupation were found within. However, the lack of debris means it is unlikely that this occupation could ever have been intensive at the site itself, though several farmsteads are known in the area.

War Ditches, again with a circular plan and a defensive bank and ditch, has been totally destroyed by quarrying. From 1894 archaeologists excavated small areas in impossibly difficult conditions (**3**). Early prehistoric features and artefacts from the site have already been mentioned, and Roman and Anglo-Saxon use will be discussed in later sections, for its position on top of a chalk spur overlooking fens to the north and the broad valley of the Cam to the east make it an important location for defence, trade and burial monuments. Smaller than Arbury Camp, the enclosed area is about 55m in diameter, with a ditch up to 8m wide, 3.5m deep, and an enclosed area of less than 5 acres. Early Iron Age sherds were noted in the lowest levels of the ditch and were perhaps derived from occupation before the ditches were dug. The upper layers had Late Iron Age pottery and many skeletons which the excavators described graphically as charred and dismembered,

4   *One of the Late Iron Age ditches on Castle Hill*

lying as if thrown into the ditch. Such bodies can be compared with those found in and around other forts, and could well be connected with scenes of fighting.

Settlements lay on gravel soils south of Cambridge, close to the river and to the main roads into the town which were already used as routeways. Early Iron Age pits and ditches were found on Hills Road in the same anti-tank trenches as the Neolithic pit noted above, a bronze razor characteristic of this period lying amongst the common finds of hand-made pottery and animal bone. Excavations of a Late Iron Age site underneath New Addenbrooke's Hospital, also on Hills Road, recovered a large rectangular enclosure, storage pits and the post-holes of a house. Another much larger Late Iron Age site seems to extend over much of the area between the other two routes into Cambridge from the south, Trumpington Road and the Cam. There have been various excavations here, but the sites were already disturbed and, being in an urban area, lack the cropmarks which could have provided an overall view of these complexes. We can see this area as one of the typical extensive Iron Age settlements with ditched fields and paddocks, small round wattle and daub houses standing amidst their fields (sometimes surrounded by their own sub-rectangular enclosure), with storage pits, granaries, and other agricultural structures. As was almost always the case, this settlement continued to be farmed without interruption well into the Roman period, with a more systematic arrangement of its fields and sounder houses constructed on the same site after Romanisation was established. The area in use stretched down to the Cam, where there was a fording place across to settlements in Grantchester. Another large site of similar date is known from the other side of Cambridge beneath the important Roman farms at Arbury.

5   *Late Iron Age pottery from a ditch on Castle Hill. Photograph: John Scott*

The major village of this Late Iron Age period included a defended enclosure on Castle Hill, and it is this site which can be seen as a true ancestor of the Roman town and all that came after it. It is reckoned to extend over at least seven hectares, stretching from the river up to the top of the hill and beyond. Dense occupation has been found throughout this area, covering a larger site than its Roman successor and with enclosures surrounded by banks, ditches and defended entrances placed to control the river crossing and the only routes out of Cambridge to the north and west (**4**). This area was extensively excavated as part of the work on the Roman town, and occupation has been recognised which covers several generations. The first settlement, founded in the first century BC, could be identified by its rectangular enclosure and its vertically-sided storage pits. The ditches were up to 2m wide and 1.2m deep, and were often recut to prolong their life. Later on there were five circular enclosures containing the walls and hearths of dwellings (**5-6**). A final phase of the pre-Roman site included a great ditch, 2m deep and 3m wide, astride the track that became the Godmanchester road. It was a long-lived feature that was recut on four occasions, and its gateway was flanked by huge posts set deep in the subsoil. It is not known whether the whole village was re-designed to lie within these defences, which are similar in size and strength to the forts at Arbury and War Ditches, or whether it was the homestead of a local chieftain and part of a still-extensive village. Judging by the number of Late Iron Age gold and silver coins found in Cambridge, mostly Catuvellaunian but

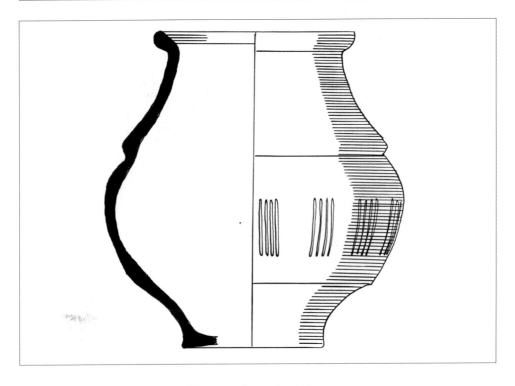

6   *A Late Iron Age pot imported from Gaul. Height: 125 mm*

with a few of the Trinovantes, the area the settlement commanded was seen as a regional centre, presumably with control of trade and tax-collection within the power-base of the dominant tribal kingdom.

All the burials of the Iron Age so far known from Cambridge belong to the wealthiest classes, and they are sufficiently numerous and widespread to give a good indication of the growing importance of the central area. The earliest of these, dating to the Middle Iron Age, is the most spectacular. Like the others it was a casual discovery with no proper recording of the grave or its contents, but at least it was seen in the ground by Baron von Hugel, curator of the University Museum of Archaeology at the time, and in a letter of 1903 he gives some details. It was in a deep pit at the back of St Mark's church in Newnham and consisted of the contracted body of a man with three bronze brooches on his chest, one of which was set with plaques of white shell, a highly decorated bronze bracelet on his arm, four bronze rings whose position on the body is not known, and a circular object fixed to chains which may have been some sort of horse-fitting (**7**). The site may well have been marked by a mound as it was reused for burial in Anglo-Saxon times. Later burials were generally found during gravel digging, but only the complete pots found with them were kept. We can infer that urns from Chesterton, Newmarket Road and Sturbridge Common were deposited as grave goods, and two amphorae, originally containers for imported wine or oil, are also known — one from Trumpington and one from Jesus College garden. These probably accompanied the kind of princely burial more

7   *Brooch and bangle from an Iron Age princely burial at Newnham Croft*

often found in the Catuvellaunian heartlands of Hertfordshire and Essex, especially around Colchester and Welwyn. They are a good illustration not only of the trading links existing with the Roman world, but also of how aspects of Roman culture were already appreciated and assimilated into the rituals of feasting and death for the higher classes in the period before the Roman invasion.

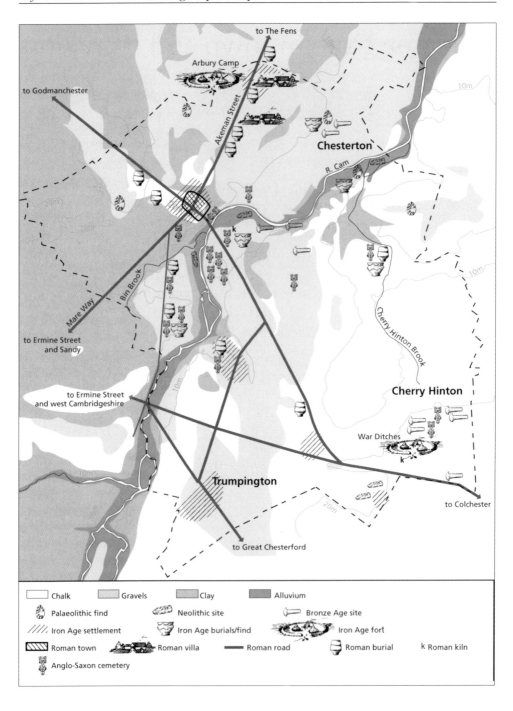

8   *Prehistoric, Roman and early Anglo-Saxon sites in Cambridge. Map drawn by Sarah Wroot*

2 The Roman town and its region

The Iron Age centre on the hill fulfilled the main criteria Romans had for a fort and a town; a defensive position commanding a major river crossing, a meeting-place of several roads, and the interface of a variety of agricultural regions, and so it was rapidly adopted by the new powers. Changes in the layout of the settlement were made soon after the Conquest and not long after this (possibly following Boudicca's revolt in AD60/61) a fort was built. Within and around this small country town there grew up potteries, metal-working sites and other local industries to serve the inhabitants and those who came to shop or trade, suburban villas were built for people who could afford a large house in the country, and cemeteries were established along the roads out of town for the dead of all classes.

In the eighteenth century the antiquarian William Stukeley explored Cambridge and was able to see many archaeological features that no longer survive, though he inevitably muddled up earthworks of later date with Roman remains. 'I have' he wrote, '... traced out the vestiges of that city ... without any difficulty; being an oblong square, which was walled about and ditched ... Then the west side of the ditch runs on the outside of the late Mr Ketil's house (Kettles Yard), and turns quite on the outside of the town, on the north'. Sadly there is nothing now to see of these remains, but between 1956 and 1986 much of the area within the Roman town was redeveloped, and local archaeologists took the opportunity to carry out excavations almost every year in this time, most of them led by John Alexander and Joyce Pullinger. In the 1990s yet more work was needed, especially just north of the town, and this was mainly carried out by the Cambridge Archaeological Unit.

The development of the town

The fate of the Late Iron Age inhabitants of the hill-top site is not known, but most could have stayed and there are plenty of other sites in the area where farmers, craftsmen and merchants could make a living. Burials found from the first century of occupation prove that the Iron Age aristocracy kept much wealth, even if their seats of power had to move. Certainly this centre did change quite rapidly, unlike rural sites where major alterations are not usually apparent for at least half a century. It would not have been in the conquerors' interest to leave any native stronghold unaltered, and official control of the area by the new power was expressed in the way the last Iron Age enclosures were immediately replaced by a new layout of ditches. Finds from these ditches include Roman brooches and a pottery lamp dating to Claudius' reign (AD41-54), so the impact of non-luxury imports occurred virtually immediately. Proper water supplies, independent of the river at the foot of the hill, were needed, and a well of this date has been excavated that was deeper than the 6 metre explorations could reach. It was timber-lined as far down as chalk bed-rock, and below this, foot-holes were cut.

The ditched enclosures were probably designed to protect an army staging post half way (and a comfortable walking distance) between the forts at Great Chesterford and Godmanchester. Then, when it was realised that southern England might not always be docile in its acceptance of the more unpleasant aspects of Roman rule and was in fact capable of the most bloodthirsty and effective rebellion, a small rectangular fort at Cambridge was one of the many military constructions designed to ensure the *Pax Romana* would not be disturbed again. Cambridge's situation near to the rebellious Icenian territories was perhaps considered particularly sensitive, and there may already have been some intentions to make more use of apparently wasteful expanses of the neighbouring Fenland. The fort that was built most probably occupied a site lying near the present Shire Hall, where trenches 2m deep and 3.6m wide were observed, although at another site just north of New Hall military-style ditches and dumps of pottery of this period have been excavated and it is possible this was the first fortress. A wide, partly cobbled, area around the fort was kept empty, with rubbish and latrine pits sited beyond. No domestic buildings were allowed until the end of the first century, and much of the old Iron Age town continued to be deserted at this time. The fort was kept in repair during this time, and the ditch was recut on at least one occasion. The first huts away from the fort have only recently been found, on the south-west of the hill-slope around Storeys Way.

Early in the second century AD Roman Cambridge emerged as the urban centre of a wide region, and its planning reflected this civilian role. First of all, the obsolete military site was reorganised. The whole area was levelled, the fort ditches being filled in and compacted and depressions left from Iron Age features topped up with rubbish-filled topsoil. A particularly dense settlement was designed in the north-west quarter, where there was a grid of streets. The houses along these streets were small one-roomed rectangular buildings, the largest of which measured 6m by 4m. Their walls were of wattle and daub with timber frames of two designs; either supported on sill-beams or by a series of large upright posts. Most must have had thatched roofs, but some were tiled, and a few had cement floors. One sign of elegance in quite a few of them was lime-plaster on interior walls, painted with patterns in many colours. There was generally a central hearth, but much of the cooking and other household activities took place outside in the large (about 10m by 12m) yards, enclosed by ditches or fences, that surrounded each house. Here there were wooden shelters, ovens, hearths and fire-pits, and light structures that were perhaps used for pig-sties, chicken coops, animal pens, hay-stores etc, for a population that still had strong rural roots. One deep scoop in a yard can be seen as a form of barbecue, for it had upright posts to support a spit, and was filled with ash and charcoal, on which had been left a lidded platter filled with mussels **(9)** and a bowl still containing the remains of a hare. These yards were gravelled or cobbled in places, presumably growing herbs and vegetables in others in cottage-garden fashion. Density of settlement was evidently low, with large empty areas away from street frontages. Many rubbish pits and wells (usually lined with timber) belong to this period.

9   *A lidded platter containing about thirty mussel shells, left over from a Roman barbecue.*
     Diameter: 210 mm. Photograph: John Scott

Settlement on the western side was less dense, with just a scatter of buildings which were generally more elaborately and substantially built. One, which may have been a wayside pub or inn for it was near the crossing of the two main roads and had a number of sherds of amphorae in the fill of its cellar, lay partly beneath the Isaac Newton public house. Its deep cellar was lined to a height of 800mm with horizontal planks nailed to upright posts. The walls of the building were plastered and then painted with blue and white stripes and designs based on plants, and the roof was tiled. It was destroyed by fire, perhaps during re-decoration for lumps of glauconite, used as green pigment for wall-painting, were found along with nails, daub, brick, tile, oyster shell and other burnt remains.

The largest building in the town was sited next to Akeman Street, on the extreme northern edge, looking over the open ground which fell away to the lower levels of Arbury and the Fens. It may have been a *mansio*, or official inn for travellers, especially those on government business. Its thick walls were made of limestone blocks, the only masonry structure to be found within the town, and central heating was supplied by a hypocaust. The warmed floor above this was painted in red and cream. Sherds found in its destruction layers included many second-century fine wares that would have been used for eating and drinking (**10**).

During the third century there were years of recession in much of the Roman world, and in Cambridge these difficulties are reflected in a state of dereliction followed by drastic change. In some parts of the town, sites that had once been residential were used as gravel quarries or for rubbish pits. However, a number of these pits were extremely

10   *Sherds of samian ware decorated with gladiators and hunting scenes, found in the early Roman town*

large and were dug in an organised fashion, with straight sides and flat bottoms. Compacted into them were great quantities of refuse, as if the town was taking every care to keep other areas tidy and habitable, and it is possible that people were simply leaving the old centre of the town in favour of fresh and more spacious sites nearby. Scattered settlements outside the main settlement have been noted in several areas, such as Madingley Road, where large-scale excavation has never been possible. It seems from recent discoveries that an area of at least 49 acres (20ha) could have been in use north of the river and that there was also widespread use of land to the south. Sites by the river, suitable for uses involved with river-trade, produce signs of use in this period whenever land is excavated (**11**).

The settlement may have been large, but it lacked any public or official buildings, and there are no signs of real urban life. Even the pottery kilns do not appear to have operated at this time. There are no evident breaks in occupation of the town, but its organisation must have changed considerably during these years of civilian use, with activity at an especially low level in the late third and early fourth centuries. However, roads and cemeteries were still very much in use, and the overall pattern of settlement did not change.

The Romans made use of trackways that had been used for generations, particularly the four roads that converged near the river-crossing which led to the Fens in the north, to the Mare Way and Icknield Way in the south, to the tribal capital of the Catuvellauni at Colchester, and along a ridgeway to the west. The Romans paved parts of these tracks with gravel and cobbles, at least within the town itself, and added side-ditches where drainage required a raised camber. Later on, construction of long-lasting buildings and neatly-designed side-streets kept the roads constrained within narrow routes, unlike the muddy tracks and drove-roads of earlier times. In the fourth century the routes were firmly fixed, for roads could only enter the town by the four gateways that pierced walls that were built

11   *A beaker decorated with a running hare, made in the Nene Valley kilns and found within the later Roman town. Height: 80 mm. Photograph: John Scott*

at that time. Several stretches of such streets have been found in excavations (sometimes with wheel-ruts still visible) or have been spotted in builders' trenches. The Fen road (later known as Akeman Street) in particular was traced for a considerable distance. It was made of matched pebbles laid close together on the natural soil, and in its first-century phase was about 11m wide with a pronounced camber and ditches on either side. Its third-century replacement was narrower and had no ditches.

Turbulent events in the Empire eventually forced Cambridge, one of the last towns to surround itself with a wall, to reorganise itself within proper defences. The complete line of these is still not known, but they have been discovered in enough places for the

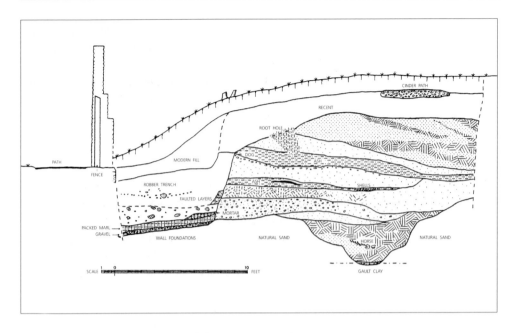

12   A section through the Roman defences at Mount Pleasant

conjectural line shown to be fairly reliable, and it can be seen that an area of about ten hectares was enclosed. They consisted of a stone wall with a bank behind it and a ditch in front **(12)**. The ditch was about 12m wide and as much as 4m deep in places. Its bank, excavated on Mount Pleasant, was about 10m wide, and survived to a height of 2.5m. The line of it here was not quite the present slope (this was created by later quarrying) but was a short distance behind this, in the gardens of houses along the top of the slope. A road ran between this bank and the walls. The stone walls themselves, which have been located in recent years on Mount Pleasant, Castle Court and under Kettles Yard extension, were 2-3m in width, made of Barnack limestone mixed with clunch blocks, flint nodules and bonding tiles, and included four gates. The West Gate has been excavated at the corner of Mount Pleasant and Albion Row. It had rectangular towers which projected in front of the town-wall, and a guardroom recessed behind it. The South Gate probably lies beneath St. Giles' church, where footings were noted during rebuilding of the church in the nineteenth century. When Sheraton House, on the Castle Court complex, was built in 1986 the robbed-out remains of the gate leading out to the Fens were found, partly overlying the *mansio*. During the same development the position of the northern gate on the road to Godmanchester, was located, but it had been hopelessly disturbed by later pits and the refurbishment of the defensive ditch during the Civil War in the seventeenth century. The wall near this point had been seen by the antiquarian, John Bowtell in 1804, and he described 'a very ancient wall...near to the turn-pike gate...the materials in the foundation of this wall consisted of flinty pebbles, fragments of Roman bricks, and ragstone so cemented that prodigious labour with the help of pick-axes etc. was required to separate them'.

Building these defences gave Cambridge, very late in the day, the status of a Roman small town. Their design must have been by an Imperial or provincial power, not a local decision, for the layout crossed many existing buildings (in one, the fire had just gone out in its hearth), whilst taking in one quarter close to the river for administrative rather than strategic motives. At the same time that these defences were built, the density of settlement increased and the town was tidied up and reorganised to suit both its confined space and its importance as part of an overall strategy to protect Roman Britain against the many threats then becoming apparent. It is possible that the town was garrisoned like the Saxon Shore forts around the coast of south-eastern Britain, which stretched as far north as Brancaster in Norfolk. In this role it could have acted to prevent access up the river from the sea, and could also have played a part in defending the Icknield Way routes across country from the eastern sea-board, both of which were eventually used by early Anglo-Saxon settlers. If this was indeed the case, there is a good chance that the very early Anglo-Saxon burials in St John's cricket field (below) could be the graves of Germanic mercenaries brought in to man the defences. Roads were repaired in this fourth-century phase, though on a humbler scale than their second-century predecessors. Some houses continued in use, and many more were built, along with their yards, drainage ditches, rubbish pits and wells. Only on the hill-slope near the river do the accounts of discoveries made in the nineteenth and early twentieth centuries suggest that some houses were well built, with stone foundations, painted plaster walls, tiled roofs and paved floors, and it was perhaps to include such buildings that the walls stretched down the hill-side. Immediately to the south of the town, in the grounds of Magdalene College, there must have been at least one house built to particularly luxurious standards. Finds included window-glass, a pillar of Barnack stone, tesserae, and coins dating to the late fourth and early fifth century. Other houses within the town were simple wood and wattle and daub structures, as in earlier years.

Industrial sites

Towns in Roman Britain often acted as magnets for various manufacturing activities, especially pottery kilns. This is because towns provided an instant market through their own inhabitants as well as those who came from the surrounding countryside to trade, and they also gave access to wider markets through their river systems. Dirty industries, like potteries, were not normally permitted within the towns themselves, but where other conditions were right (ie there were sources of fuel and clay, and the transport system was good) it was very common for them to grow up nearby. At Cambridge, small potteries have been found close to and even within the town, and there were much larger ones just outside.

At Cherry Hinton, on the site of the War Ditches, decorative tableware was manufactured in the first century AD, perhaps by potters who moved here from factories producing similar wares in Central Gaul (**13**). The same types of pot were also being made in the Fishbourne and St Albans areas, indicating a migration of potters in the early years of the Conquest to satisfy a new market for Romanised wares. Excavations in the early years of the twentieth century uncovered dumps of sherds in a distinctive fine whitish-buff ware, decorated with raised dots and circles, and mainly in the form of dishes and

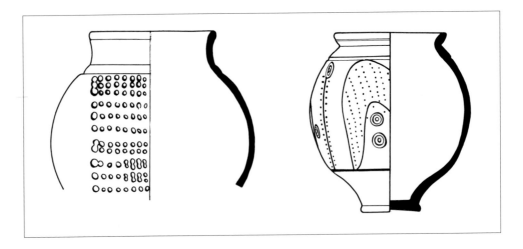

13   Pots from the Cherry Hinton kilns. Height: 85 mm

small jars or beakers. Products from these kilns had a regional distribution, the furthest distance their sherds are reported being Snape in Suffolk, about sixty miles away. Later, on a different part of the site, a small, circular up-draught kiln with a central pedestal was excavated, probably also belonging to the first century AD. The pottery produced here was mostly jars and platters in a well-fired orange-brown or buff fabric, in forms reminiscent of Late Iron Age predecessors and unlike the obvious Roman forms. These potters may have been using Roman technology to provide for traditional local tastes, and they may themselves have been local potters who were learning new techniques.

Later potteries have been found close to the town, on the opposite side of the river near Jesus Lane. Kiln debris and wasters date to the third century, the types of pot being mainly narrow-necked grey ware jars (**14**) with a light grey silvery slip, not a particularly fine ware but much superior to the crude storage jars made north of Cambridge at Horningsea. Other large-scale kilns stretched down the Cam valley between Milton and Cambridge, making a whole variety of coarsewares. It was only in the fourth century that pottery was made in the town, when there were two kilns, one apparently making grey and black indented beakers.

In the first phase of Roman use of the hill-top, before the fort was built, there were two iron-smelting furnaces on Pound Hill. In one, the domed base of a furnace about 2m in diameter was surrounded by slag and charcoal. Only the scorched bottom and the run-off channel of the other furnace remained. During the life of the fort one very large pit was filled with ash and charcoal with slag and iron bloom in the lowest levels. There were also pieces of slag in various other pits, indicating smithing for the needs of soldiers and other residents.

Evidence for one specialised craft carried out within the town was the manufacture of bone pins, much used in women's elaborate hairstyles and useful in various other ways. In one of the wells dating to the second century there was a collection of partly-worked bone pins and one finished example (**colour plate 1**). A small marble stamp used for

14   *Wasters from Roman kilns in Jesus Lane*

labelling an ointment for sore eyes is a sign that specialist medical treatment was another profession practised here at this time (**colour plate 2**).

Religion

One highly unusual shrine dates to the late second century. It was a deeply cut rectangular subterranean structure 8.18 by 5m and 2m deep, with a semi-circular apse at one end. Several posts had been set into a layer of gravel at its base, supported with packing-stones and stakes and presumably themselves supporting a massive superstructure. Planks of timber had been nailed to these uprights to line the cellar. Rows of posts at one end may have been part of a staircase. Beneath the gravel floor were found the skeleton of a dog and the skull of a cow. The cellar was entirely filled with the results of some mighty conflagration, with wood ash holding over two thousand nails, iron hinges and brackets and a key. On top of the ash lay a horse with its head split open, around which were arranged six complete pots. Three small dogs lay in a triangular shape nearby, all with collars and chains made of iron links, and a bowl was set within the triangle. Another animal sacrifice close by was a cow, which lay with a sheep between its legs. The layer that covered all this seemed to consist of deliberately smashed vessels and other remains of feasts. Huge quantities of pot sherds were mostly fine table wares (samian cups and bowls, beakers and wine flagons) and there were also glass vessels and dumps of oyster shells and meat bones. Amongst this rubbish were bone pins and needles, hobnails from boots and shoes, coins, a bone flute (**15**), and the setting for a signet ring carved with the god Bacchus (**colour plate 12**). It is with the Bacchanalian rites and festivities of this god that we can best connect the events we see here. The site was forgotten, and was eventually filled with normal domestic rubbish.

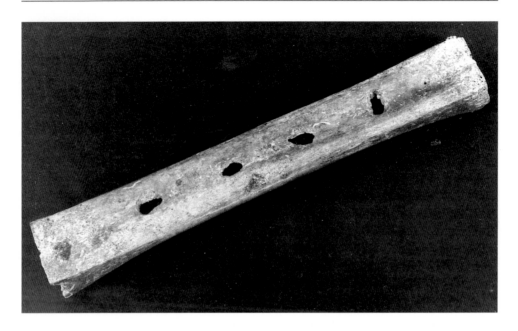

15   Bone flute or whistle from a Roman temple on Castle Hill. Length: 105 mm. Photograph: John Scott

Signs of later religious practices include a third-century pit which had a horse skeleton lying on brushwood at the bottom with two beakers, a wheel and a corroded iron object arranged around it. There are several other cases of dogs and horses placed with pots, some of which may be deliberate and ritual while others will have more mundane explanations. One particularly interesting structure, probably a temple, was a modest pentagon not far from the subterranean shrine described above (and on the site of the future churchyard of All Saints by the Castle). It was later deliberately demolished and its remains buried nearby. Votive religious objects from the town include a late Roman figurine of Venus from St. Peter's churchyard, and a bronze figurine of Mercury found near New Hall.

Burials
By Roman law all burials must be outside towns, normally on the roads leading out of them. An exception was made for young children, and fragments of many infants found their way into rubbish pits. There was one unusual cemetery for them, dating to the third/fourth centuries, in which thirteen infants were found in nine shafts, most of them lying in a wicker basket with a dog in the same pit. Shoes suitable for an older child — usually just surviving as a stain and hobnails — were found in five of the shafts. One of the babies was still wrapped in a piece of linen cloth, with a coin by its head and a complete pot nearby. Another was in a wooden coffin, and others had coins (to pay for their ferry across the River Styx into the Underworld) in their graves. Elsewhere in the town infant bones were found in several rubbish pits. It may well have been the case that these

16   Samian and glass vessels and an iron lamp from a grave at Arbury

children were originally buried near their homes, or beneath floors, and found their way into rubbish pits in later clearing-up operations. Adult burials in the town are rare, though one man whose feet had been removed was found in Castle Court with a pot of the late fourth/fifth century, the very end of the town's life.

On the roads leading out of the town graves often occur on Akeman Street to the north especially in the Arbury area. One important group was found near the Humphrey's/Arbury Road villa and farmstead described below. The earliest burials here were cremations of the second century, one furnished with a pile of seven samian vessels, four glass bottles, a glass jug, pottery flagon, and an iron lamp and its holder (**16**). This kind of feasting regalia, and the inclusion of a burning light, are typical of a group of Late Iron Age and early Roman burials in this region, and point to continued traditions despite the change to Roman control. Other cremations included a samian bowl stamped with the name of its potter, MERCATOR, and there are several with simple cooking pots.

Fourth-century burials were inhumations, generally in coffins. Most of these have no grave goods, though sometimes the hobnails of their boots survive. Inhumations from Humphrey's Road were buried in lead-lined stone coffins, one of them within a mausoleum (**17**). Two similar late Roman stone coffins were found on the Godmanchester road, also probably part of a larger cemetery. Close to one was a group of vessels and jewellery, including four glass bottles, a jet bracelet and pins, and pots for food and drink. A little further up the road, under Girton College, many burials (some of them cremations with feasting gear and lamps, others inhumations in mausolea ornamented with magnificent stone carvings) would also have belonged to residents of the town.

Cemeteries to the south of the Roman town were inevitably disturbed more by the growth of the medieval and later town, and in this area too, Anglo-Saxons used much of

17   *Roman burial in a lead and stone coffin, excavated at Arbury Road*

the land and took over the cemeteries. Evidence, therefore, tends to be scattered and inconclusive. It includes two fine glass vessels from Coldham's Common, various bodies from Newnham and from Long Road, and graves that became confused with the later Saxons at St John's cricket ground, Grange Road and at a particularly interesting cemetery along the Trumpington Road. This last example is important for it spans the Conquest period, with stamped samian plates, jugs and an amphora deposited during the first century AD. Gravel digging led to collection of 'many urns and paterae', and at least one large urn which contained cremated bone. It was still being used for cremations in the second century, and later for inhumations. The cemetery was probably marked by a barrow or other distinctive feature, for later there were Anglo-Saxon graves in the same area.

Suburban settlement

Along the course of Akeman Street, leading out to the Fens, there were many important buildings including villa complexes. Closest to the town, in the area of Arbury Road, was a range of houses in use continuously from about AD130 until after 400, uncovered by salvage excavations when new housing estates were built in the 1950s. In the latest phase one house had three rooms with painted plaster walls, (bright red, yellow, green, grey, and deep blue were used, some of it patterned to imitate panels of marble), a tiled roof, mortar floors, glass windows, underfloor heating and foundations of imported blocks of chalk. In the yard outside was a timber-lined well, its sawn oak beams still perfectly preserved, and a box of late fourth-century coins was buried. Many narrow-mouthed pits on this site were used for storage of grain, suggesting that the wealth of this family was derived from large scale and well organised agriculture.

Further along the Fen road, around King's Hedges school, another villa flourished from the second century amidst many hectares of fields and paddocks. The original site was an Iron Age farm, and the first-century Roman buildings were quite humble. Then, in the second and third centuries, there was a rectangular aisled building, probably with two-storeys, its floor paved with red, white and grey tesserae. Blocks of sculptured stone found dumped in a well nearby may have been part of this villa, or a temple connected with it (**colour plate 3**). At least a century passed before, in the fourth century, this now-ruined building was converted into a remarkably comfortable ten-roomed villa, demonstrating that wealth, confidence, security and building expertise were not lacking at this late stage of the Roman empire's life in Britain.

A Roman farmstead was built within the old War Ditches and used until the early second century. Three rectangular buildings were excavated, the largest measuring about 8 by 13 metres, the size of some villas, although its simple construction (**18**) is very different. In the fourth century, there were still flourishing farms along the valleys of the Cam and Granta, and immediately south of the river there is plentiful evidence of settlement at this period, for example from Magdalene and Sidney Sussex Colleges, Bridge Street and Market Hill. Well to the south of the town, in Trumpington, there was a rich roadside settlement with finds dating from the first to the late fourth centuries, and tiles, tesserae and general rubbish have also been found along Hills Road, the other major road into Cambridge from the south.

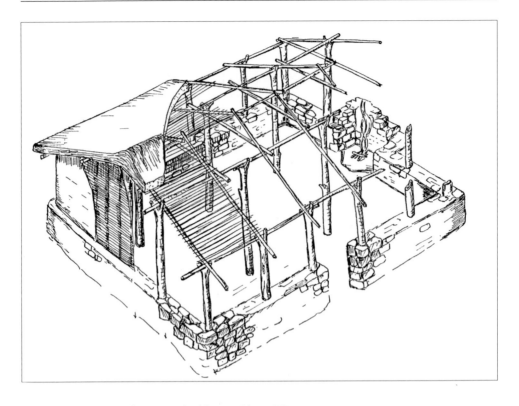

18   *Reconstruction of a Roman building at Cherry Hinton*

Over the life of Roman Cambridge, therefore, we have seen significant changes in the role and structure of the town, starting as an Iron Age urban-style settlement that was taken over by the new power for its military significance at the expense of its trade and other civilian aspects. This military presence led to the construction of a neatly-planned small town, with good roads and an excellent situation to develop as a trading centre. Minor industries, provisions for religious ceremonies, a few rich burials, and one official building, a *mansio* or inn, can be seen at this time. Between the late second and the fourth centuries this promising start came to little, although the increasing size of the settlement and the care we see taken over periodic cleaning up operations show that municipal life was not dead. External threats led authorities to take control again in the fourth century, when once more the strategic sites of the hill-top and river-crossing in the defence of the region were appreciated, the whole settlement being re-ordered in a more confined space for this new life. The end of the Roman town is a mystery that so far archaeology cannot solve. There are certainly no indications of a violent end, and no widespread burning or destruction. No definite Anglo-Saxon features or sherds were found with Roman material, though these were searched for over many years. Instead, some 15-30cm of 'black earth', as commonly found in Roman towns, overlay all the Roman features and separated them from the Saxon settlement.

3 Cemeteries and re-growth: the Anglo-Saxon period

The clear Roman pattern of town and suburbs disappeared at the beginning of this period and was replaced with scattered rural settlements that would only coalesce into villages at a late stage in the Anglo-Saxon period. Material goods that had depended on Roman trade and technology were lost and so were architectural styles, literacy and the Christian religion, to be replaced with a very different Germanic culture. This happened at some time in the early fifth century, for the Cam was a principal route into Britain from the North Sea homelands of the Anglo-Saxons. There are arguments to suggest their warriors were being used as mercenaries to protect the town in the last days of the Empire, and whether this was the case or not the importance of the site would have been well known, and control of it would have been a priority for anyone holding power in the region after the departure of the Roman legions in AD410. The Romano-British who were left to run the town without military support or other contact with the Roman world were in an impossible situation in this part of Britain. Whereas inhabitants of defensible towns such as Verulamium and those in the west country could preserve remnants of their old life-style for a few more generations, here the change was fast and final.

On the other hand, good farmland was too valuable to waste and would have been taken over and run with similar efficiency, maintaining overall settlement patterns, and communications by roads and river were still viable. The importance of Cambridge as a centre of disputed tribal powers with control of cross-country travel and North Sea migration routes was as strong as ever. We can recognise through the archaeological remains of the fifth and sixth centuries how wealth, population density and prestige were still concentrated in this area.

Despite extensive investigations within the area of the old Roman town and a century of piecemeal investigation and watching of developments elsewhere in Cambridge, no definite houses or other structures of the early Anglo-Saxon period have yet been found, although burial rituals of the early pagan years have left valuable remains. These rituals involved either inhumation or cremation in fine clothes and jewellery, with weapons and other personal items. Study of the artefacts sacrificed to the dead tell us much about the cultural and tribal affiliations of the population, how people dressed and were armed, and something of their artistic preferences, technological skills, trading contacts and wealth. The cemeteries are also statements that certain areas now truly belonged to particular groups through the relatives they buried. We know too that reusing older burial sites was extremely common, if not universal, for sites so claimed for the ancestors were a part of the struggles for dominance and land-ownership by warring tribal groups. We do not yet

19   Anglo-Saxon cremation urns from St John's cricket ground. Photographs: copyright
Cambridge University Museum of Archaeology and Anthropology

understand the relationship of cemeteries to settlements, but it was not a simple one-to-one pairing as we see later on with parish graveyards, and cemetery sites were chosen for values other than convenience. The symbolism of this is too complicated for us to follow through archaeological remains, but Cambridge and the Cam are often seen as a boundary between the emerging rival kingdoms of East Anglia and Mercia. Although in the early years the situation would have been more complicated than this, their importance is demonstrated by the way rich cemeteries cluster here on both sides of the river.

The largest cemetery was on St John's cricket field. This was principally a cremation cemetery but there were also many inhumation graves. It was in use from the fifth until the seventh century. Over one hundred urns were retrieved and deposited in the Cambridge University Museum of Archaeology and Anthropology along with other artefacts, but it was reported that 'many hundreds' more were destroyed without record. Study of the pots shows that a number of them were made at a local production centre, and that the workshops here kept stockpiles of various additives (flint and limestone chips, crushed chalk, Roman brick and broken pots) to add to local clays, along with grass and other vegetable matter. Other potters, identifiable by the design of the pots and the stamps used to decorate them, also supplied cemeteries at Girton and Barrington. One type of pot probably originated near Lackford in Suffolk, where another cemetery contains many more, and this type also occurs in Little Wilbraham cemetery (**19**). In addition to cremated remains, the urns contained grave goods, most of which were burned with the body. These were similar but not identical to grave goods left with inhumations. Bodies were cremated fully clothed, wearing jewellery and with other personal items, many of which will have been lost in the flames or during their years in the ground. Typical objects that survived in one urn include a pair of bronze brooches, fragments of bone combs, and wrist-clasps to fasten the woman's long sleeves. Another grave had amber and blue, yellow and multi-coloured glass beads, an ivory ring and an iron key. Another had a brooch, fragments of a glass vessel and much ironwork. Small and even miniature objects were often made to accompany cremations. There are two pairs of miniature iron shears from St John's, and also knives and combs. Oddly-sized weapons include three very small spears and part of an impractically small iron boss from the centre of a wooden shield.

Inhumation graves also featured jewellery with women and weapons with men. Items now surviving include about 48 brooches, wrist-clasps, and a great many glass and amber beads with women, and seven spears and three shield-bosses with men. A particularly well-equipped woman's grave had a square-headed gilded brooch along with two round ones, amber beads, very decorative wrist-clasps, and an iron knife and latch-lifter. Other items from this cemetery include pins, combs, tweezers, knives, buckles, silver pendants and finger-rings, spindle-whorls, and a strap-end which still had linen braid dyed white, blue-green and indigo attached to it. More ornate items were an elaborate bronze buckle set with garnets, five chip-carved and gilded belt plates, and a sword pommel, though no blade was recorded. These male items were the only sign of real wealth in this cemetery, all other objects being part of the normal dress of the Anglian population. One woman, otherwise traditionally dressed, wore a Roman brooch which must have been found in working order, Roman coins were perforated and used on necklaces, and fragments of Roman bottle glass and many decorated samian sherds were collected from graves. It is not possible to fully disentangle all items used as grave goods from evidence for Roman occupation in the area, but there is no doubt that many had been collected as curios and were buried as treasured belongings.

Other burials north of the river may be outliers of St John's, or may be from separate cemeteries entirely. Brooches and other artefacts suggestive of burials extend in a wide band from Milton Road, Magdalene Bridge and Madingley Road to Grange Road and Newnham. Here they were found on both sides of Barton Road, close to the Iron Age warrior burial and Roman graves described above. Decorated sherds from cremation urns have been found, but the majority of these are inhumation burials of the sixth century (**20**). Artefacts collected are mainly brooches, beads, and spears, but one interesting grave had brooches, beads, wrist-clasps and a bunch of bronze spangles whose only possible use was being shaken to make a pleasant noise.

South of the river, objects from graves in the same Anglian traditions have been collected throughout the area later enclosed by the King's Ditch. Sites include Jesus Lane, Clare and Trinity Colleges, Sidney Street, Petty Cury, and three shield bosses with spears, knives and cremations from Rose Crescent. From surrounding areas, sites occur on Coldham's Common along with Roman and Iron Age burials, Newmarket Road and Mill Road cemetery. Further out, the Roman and Iron Age cemetery at Trumpington was used again. Finds from here include a fifth-century brooch, similar to a pair from St John's cricket field, and a crystal ball in a bronze sling, an object connected with magical properties, as well as brooches, wrist-clasps and spears. A particularly interesting cemetery of the seventh century reused the Bronze Age barrows at War Ditches. One of the burials was lying in a wooden bed with iron fittings, a strange ritual known from two other sites in Cambridgeshire and six from elsewhere in England. With this were found another crystal ball in a sling, a glass and silver necklace, two combs, knives and a spear head.

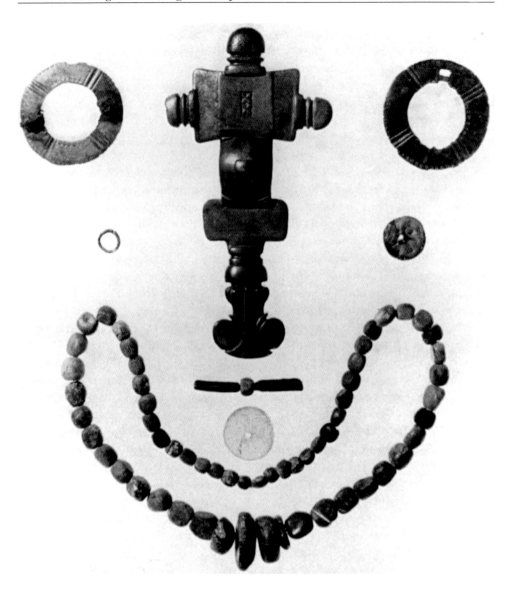

20   *Anglo-Saxon grave goods from Newnham Croft*

Re-creating urban life; an historical outline

At the end of the seventh century there is the first written reference to the town. In AD695, a few years after St Etheldreda foundress of the monastery at Ely died, her sister and successor sent messengers to 'a little ruined city called *Grantacaestir'* for a stone coffin to bury her in, and there one (obviously of Roman date) was found. The walled town would still have been quite recognisable at this time, probably still the focus and regional centre for organised activities of tribal life. Evidence for proto-urban activity in this early period includes concentrations of coins from various kingdoms which point to markets and other inter-regional economic functions. Its geographical position was becoming more significant in these years, for the kingdoms of East Anglia and Mercia were fighting for land and supremacy, and Cambridgeshire to the east of the Cam was a battle zone. Devils Dyke seems to be accepted as a boundary in the later Anglo-Saxon period, but in earlier years control of this bridging point of the Cam was crucial. Cambridge itself was also the key to economic power, through its situation at the point where foreign goods from around the North Sea could be imported. Its position on a frontier also meant that it was able to take advantage of a variety of markets with minimal control from the centres, often a good situation for urban growth.

In the eighth century the town was under the control of the powerful Mercian king Offa, well known for his definition of clear defensible frontiers and the creation of defended urban centres or *burhs,* where economic life could flourish under military protection and where a concentration of citizens was useful for manning defences in times of trouble. Ready-made fortifications in the form of Roman walls and the importance of both encouraging and taxing trade from the North Sea were additional attractions. It is thought that Offa's Mercian town was essentially on the north-western side of the river, with a market place by the northern gates on a site known in the middle ages as Ashwyke Cross. A ditch which was navigable to St Giles in the thirteenth century and which protected an area by the river later known as the *Armeswerch* may have been dug at this time to protect shipping.

A reeve or alderman, who exercised power on behalf of the king, was probably housed in a ditched enclosure near the market. Ditches that perhaps defined this enclosure, still called *Le Sale* or Sale Piece in the twelfth century, were excavated in 1983. It is highly likely that a church was also built at this time, of which the only traces are the Anglo-Saxon grave slabs described below. This church may have been on the site of St Giles or All Saints by the Castle, or on some lost site within the castle area. It was also almost certainly Offa who built a bridge a short distance from where the Roman one had stood. To do this needed an authority that was secure in its control of both banks of the river and to which economic development was more important than a defensive boundary. Because of this bridge, when Cambridge next enters the written record in the Anglo-Saxon Chronicle for 875, it is known for the first time as *Granta Brycge.*

In the ninth century all the Anglo-Saxon kingdoms were once more under threat, this time from Scandinavian invaders who began with casual piratical raids but progressed into wholesale invasion. As in early Anglo-Saxon times, East Anglia was highly vulnerable to this invasion, and was overrun by an occupying army. In 875, the Anglo-Saxon Chronicle describes how the Danish kings 'went from Repton to Cambridge with a great host, and

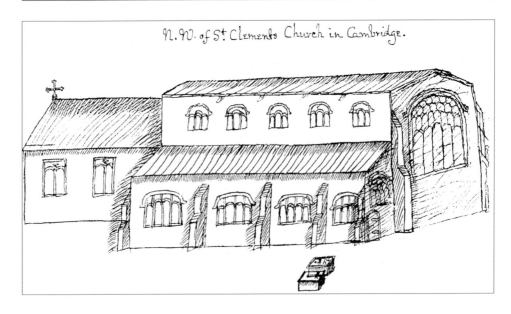

N.W. of St Clements Church in Cambridge.

21   *St Clement's church, drawn by William Cole in the eighteenth century*

remained there a year'. Five year later the Danes are described as occupying East Anglia, whilst continuing to fight with Alfred of Wessex for the rest of England. In 886 Alfred and Guthrum, leader of the Danes, made peace and Cambridge became part of the Danelaw.

The succeeding years of Danish rule had lasting effects on the developing town of Cambridge and the surrounding countryside. Like earlier powers, they needed a well-defended trading position and an administrative centre for the region, and their new base appears to have been an area just south of the river which they defended with ditches, known in later years as *Hulmum*, after the Danish *Homr*, or 'higher dry ground amidst the marshes'. This area covers the parishes of Holy Sepulchre and St Clement's. St Clement's is a Danish name, and its riverside location is typical for Danish worship following conversion to Christianity (**21**). The new Danish ditches joined up with the *Armeswerch* on the northern bank to provide a fortified inland port. It can also be argued that it was the Danes who created the county of Cambridgeshire, with Cambridge as the administrative centre, although it is difficult to disentangle aspects of their administrative reforms from those of the next century.

Another phase began in 917 when Edward the Elder, son of Alfred, reconquered what had become known as the Danelaw. He too needed efficient government, and it was most probably his optimistic decision to expand the southern town and to define it with the King's Ditch. We cannot yet be certain how much suburban development existed in Late Saxon times, but if we are correct in assigning the churches of Little St Mary's, St Botolph's, and Great St Andrew's to this phase, then it is highly likely that the communities they were built for were already established. Further Saxon settlements also existed at Barnwell and Newnham Croft (then a daughter-hamlet of Grantchester) as well as in the villages of Chesterton, Trumpington and Cherry Hinton. The existence of substantial post-Conquest manor houses north of the river (now the School of Pythagoras) and south of Trumpington Gate (later to be given to the Gilbertines and to the Friars of the Sack) may also be indicators of manorial development in earlier years. Otherwise the King's Ditch was not only a custom's barrier and a defence in times of trouble (in which role it was rather a failure), but was also the limit of possible development until Cambridge's open fields were enclosed in the nineteenth century.

A further time of trouble came in the early eleventh century, as the Viking forces renewed themselves for the invasions that would put the Danish king Cnut on the English throne. The first East Anglian town burnt was Norwich, after which the Viking forces were defeated. A few years later they were back. Men of Cambridgeshire are recorded as standing bravely against them when the East Angles fled, but nevertheless 'the land three months ravaged and burned; and they even went into the wild fen, and they destroyed men and cattle, and burned throughout the fens: Thetford they burned and Cambridge'. As usual, the King's Ditch and other defences in Cambridge seem to have been useless, but development of the town was not apparently affected, or at least recovery was rapid.

Agriculture

Important developments in Cambridge before the Norman Conquest included the creation of two systems of open fields, one paying tithes to St Giles and St Clement's, the other tithing to churches of the tenth-century lower town, south-east of the river. These fields were farmed in strips, just as they were in villages from Saxon times until Enclosure in the nineteenth century. This agricultural base was to remain important to the life of the town, and the wide green areas we still have around the central settlement are mostly a relic of these Saxon field systems (**23**).

Trade and Industry

There were three mills on the river, and some modest evidence for other commercial activities. For example, there was a mint to produce silver coins for the region on the king's behalf from 975 onwards, and coins of Alfred, St Edmund, Edgar, Ethelred II and a mid ninth-century French king occur, and there are documentary references to foreign merchants trading in the town. One important feature of town life that was lacking, as it was in later times, was an industrial base. Exceptions are traces of late Saxon (or early Norman) kilns, found during excavations in both the upper and lower towns, and the carving of stone crosses and grave covers with elaborate plaitwork decoration. This business used limestone from Barnack, north of Peterborough, and its products were exported to many villages in southern Cambridgeshire.

The town plan and its buildings (22)

Many churches were being built in the late Saxon period, the only buildings in stone in the town at this time, although medieval rebuilding was so thorough that it is impossible to be sure which churches did originate before the Norman Conquest, apart from the magnificent example of St Benet's, whose Saxon chancel, nave and tower are still in use (**24**). Others which are good candidates for Saxon origins are Little St Mary (originally St Peter's) and St Edward the King and Martyr's (dedicated to an obscure late Saxon boy-

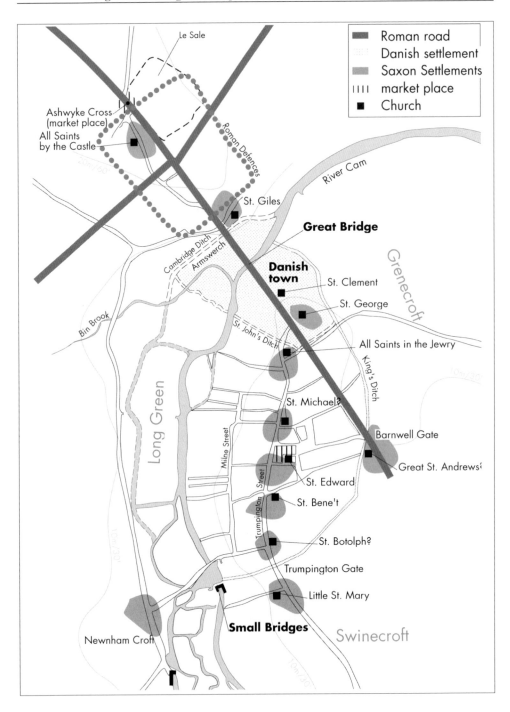

22   *Later Anglo-Saxon Cambridge. Map drawn by Sarah Wroot*

23 *The open fields around Cambridge, drawn by Jeremy Haslam in the* Proceedings of Cambridge Antiquarian Society 72, *1984*

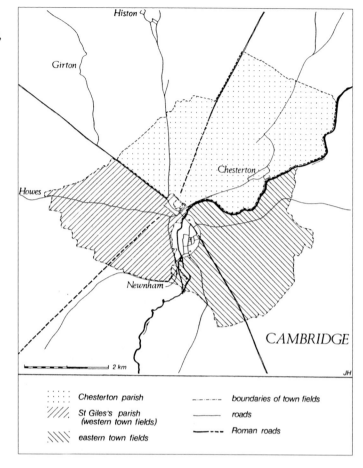

king and in which were found fragments of decorative stone coffins, probably used for their priests in the early eleventh century), All Saints in the Jewry (now demolished), St George's (lost in the twelfth century, when Holy Sepulchre was built in its churchyard), St Clement's, St Botolph's (whose dedication and location are typically Saxon), and another church on Castle Hill, which may have been All Saints by the Castle (itself lost after the middle ages). St Michael's and St Andrew the Great (on the site of the present Victorian church of the same name) may also have originated in this period. The most interesting case is perhaps St Giles (**25**), which still contains an eleventh-century arch that was moved from the church that stood on the site until 1875, and which is on the boundary of the Roman town north of the river. Its foundation was claimed by Picot, the sheriff of Cambridge, who took it over and created a priory there in 1092, but this probably means that he seized an existing minster whose priests served a wide area before parish churches were universal, and gave it to Norman Canons Regular who had similar functions. Two stone coffins containing skeletons were found in 1795 beneath the ramparts of the castle, and more coffins with their decorative lids and marker stones, and a cross with similar decoration, turned up during further works in 1810 (**26**). The siting of these discoveries is probably too far north to belong to St Giles, and they may belong

24   St Benet's church, drawn by William Cole in the eighteenth century

to All Saints by the Castle, which went out of use in the thirteenth century, or to a church in the area of the castle that was subsequently lost. It is tempting to ascribe St Peter's also to the Saxon period, as it stands just across the Roman road from St. Giles, also on or adjacent to the walls, but so far there is no evidence earlier than the Norman period.

Archaeological recording work that has led to discoveries of Anglo-Saxon artefacts from the lower town took place when two energetic students, Martin Biddle and Peter Addyman, explored construction holes dug during major developments in the 1950s and '60s, and Anglo-Saxon remains were sought during excavations in the upper town. It was clear that it was the lower town that was much the most populous and important, and this has been confirmed by larger-scale excavations in the 1990s. Archaeological evidence supports the suggestion that the area between the market and St Benet's church was the most densely settled, but it also confirms the presence of early settlement outside the two gates. Many pits containing Saxo-Norman sherds of St Neot's and Thetford wares were excavated under Bradwell's Court and Post Office Terrace (just south of the present church) outside Barnwell Gate near to Great St Andrew's, and eleventh-century pottery was excavated in the churchyard of Little St Mary. Saxo-Norman wares are also found throughout the area bounded by the King's Ditch, with concentrations between the market and St Benet's. There is also evidence for life in the upper town in the years of Danish and later occupation. Silver coins of 905 and 915 were found in a pit with late Saxon pottery and animal bones, and a scatter of rubbish pits and two enclosures may also

25   The old church of St Giles, demolished in 1870

belong to the Danish period. Several eleventh-century ditches, gullies, pits, post-holes, wells and a hut must be pre-Conquest, for the only features later than 1068 belonged to the castle. Enclosures laid out at this time were too irregular to be systematically laid-out urban plots, and seem to be more horticultural in nature.

The late Saxon town had Trumpington Street as its main road for, like virtually all the villages in this region, the area of main settlement was laid out *away* from the major highway, which in this case continued to be the old Roman road. There were crossing-places of the river at the Great Bridge and at Small Bridges, an ancient ford at the southern end of the town crossed by a road leading to Newnham, Grantchester, and other villages on that bank of the Cam. Along this high street churches were built at road intersections at approximately 100 metre intervals and the market place was set in the centre. Although the main area of the late Saxon town was bounded by the King's Ditch it would not have filled all of this area at this time, but is more likely instead to have consisted of several separate communities, each about the same size as a village in the countryside and each with its own parish church and road network. These communities were probably the ten wards into which Cambridge was divided in Domesday Book. Of these communities, that on Market Hill (still the site of Cambridge's market) would have had the most obviously urban characteristics, probably served by St Edward's church unless there was an unrecognised predecessor to Great St Mary's. Eleventh-century buildings are hard to locate in this area as they are about 4m below present street levels, but they do occur

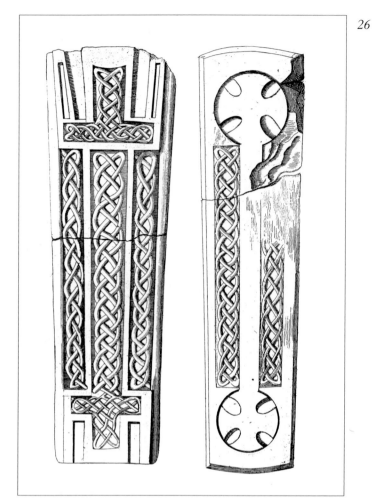

26   *Anglo-Saxon grave slabs found beneath Cambridge Castle*

regularly whenever such trenches are dug. It is also worth noting that the earliest parishes in central Cambridge have been described as an intricate jig-saw puzzle, with churches and cross-roads at their heart. Although our first record of these is nineteenth century they clearly reflect a far more ancient arrangement which one would normally expect to be Anglo-Saxon.

The origins of Cambridge are often described as 'dual', ie deriving from two main centres based either side of the river, but this picture of scattered centres fits the archaeological, architectural and historical evidence more closely, and is also similar to the ways Saxon villages developed as discrete settlements around churches and ancient routeways. Cambridge therefore, despite the administrative and market functions given to it by either Danish or late Saxon kings, was more a collection of small village-like communities than a proto-urban centre, and in many ways this is what it remained.

4 The Castle

When William the Conqueror took England by force in 1066 there was no knowing that his conquest was to be permanent, for England was a warlike nation which had seen various royal families and foreign powers come and go in that same century. Only luck, ruthless destruction of the Saxon landowning class in favour his own followers, and the building of castles to control centres of population and power gave him the chance to found a dynasty that would last. The type of castle he built was already common in his homeland in northern France, and a few examples had been built in England by knights of Edward the Confessor, but the notion of controlling one's own population by the use of defended strong-points rather than using fortifications such as burh walls to give one's own people protection against raiders and invaders was wholly new.

William and his followers can have had little idea of the detailed geography of England but they knew that its administrative systems were based on the shires, and that these were governed from the shire towns. These towns already had their own stone or earthwork defences, often reusing what the Romans had left, and they were usually sited strategically with regard to river crossings, major routeways, and naturally defensive positions. It was therefore a simple matter to order the construction of ditched enclosures within the Saxon defences and to use them as a base for armed garrisons, with Norman sheriffs replacing Saxon earls. In the time scales given for building such fortifications it is unlikely that motte and bailey castles were erected in the first instance, but instead were probably simple ring-works and timber towers, strengthened by the addition of earthen mounds in due course.

The first few years of the Conquest were filled with castle-building campaigns to consolidate control over each region through which William passed. He started in the south and then, after an expedition to York in 1068, returned to London via Lincoln, Huntingdon and Cambridge, ordering the construction of a castle in each. All of these were within the defended quarters of the Saxon towns and, although not the most populous areas, were by no means uninhabited. Lincoln saw a massive 166 properties destroyed to make way for its castle, and in Cambridge, though the hill-top was now the quieter area, 27 houses were pulled down. The resulting mottes still stand, in Cambridge being the only complete element we can now see of the successive fortifications built here for more than five centuries afterwards. Cambridge castle was left in the possession of sheriff Picot, a hate figure who is described in a contemporary chronicle kept by the monks of Ely, the *Liber Eliensis,* as 'a hungry lion, a ravening wolf, a filthy hog'. With him would be an armed and mounted force, and he had automatic support from all the knights who were given confiscated land in the shire. The castle itself was counted a royal possession, as it was to remain. Its sheriff could control and draw revenue from the town,

27   *An engraving of Cambridge Castle in 1730, showing the motte and the gatehouse, drawn by Samuel and Nathaniel Buck*

but the castle was not part of Cambridge but was instead in the parish of Chesterton. Together with three churches, St Giles', St Peter's and All Saints by the Castle, and the enclosure of Sale Piece, it covered most of the area of the old upper town, further restricting the chances of recovery of town life there.

The castle itself, a motte and bailey from early in the Norman period, consisted of a flattened cone standing about 17m above the ground surface as it falls away to the south, with a wooden tower, a deep water-filled ditch around its base, and a wet ditch and bank surmounted with a stout fence forming a bailey in front of it. Its north-eastern side made use of the old Roman town-ditch. The bailey was about two hectares in extent and would have contained all the buildings needed by a permanent garrison and sheriff, including rudimentary judicial and administrative buildings for the shire. It was sited near the end of a promontory of high ground which meant that some of its height could be achieved by scarping the natural hill-side, and from it there were (and still are) wide views in three directions: across the Fens, southern Cambridgeshire, and the commercial town and its river. Continual funding for the upkeep of the castle, as for the bridge across the Cam, was paid for by levies on villages in south-west Cambridgeshire, a hang-over from the defence of the burh in Anglo-Saxon times (**27** and **colour plate 4**) .

For the next two hundred years the castle had no trouble in its primary purpose of keeping the town under royal control, and it was also kept busy as a prison, the site of monthly courts, and the offices for the sheriff's tax-collecting and other duties. However it was obviously no use at all for two other functions expected of a royal castle; protecting against military attack and being a royal residence when visits to Cambridge were made. In military terms it was of only peripheral importance to the king in the many campaigns

28   *Edward I's gatehouse in 1808*

fought in these years. It may have been used as a base for the fight against Hereward the Wake in the Isle of Ely in 1070 but was not significant in this important war, and it failed to protect Cambridge from damaging rebel attacks in the later eleventh, twelfth and thirteenth centuries. It was perhaps because of these disasters that Edward I included Cambridge in his great castle-building programme. Work in Cambridge, which was to cost over £2500, was on nothing like the scale of his castles in Wales, where expenditure on nine castles came to at least £80,000, but it was vastly more ambitious than anything that went before. Up to that time all the defences and buildings were of earth, wood and thatch, with a garrison that does not seem to have exceeded twenty men. But Edward's new stone castle was intended to provide serious security in the face of sophisticated siege warfare, and it was only by historical accident that the violent events of the next century, including the Wars of the Roses, took place elsewhere so the fortifications here went unused.

Building works lasted from 1283 to 1299. Detailed accounts were kept, so we can see that a hundred men were working here most of the time, that stone was brought from Peterborough, hard clunch came from Harlton and softer clunch for lime came from Reach. The new defences consisted of a tower on the motte, the Great Gate on Castle Street, three corner towers (one of which was used as the prison), a barbican gate standing opposite the Great Gate on the east side of Castle Street and reached by a drawbridge (this being later replaced in stone) over the moat, a curtain wall of stone with clunch footings and a thatched covering, and a substantial water-filled moat that ran along the present route of Castle Street and beneath the houses and gardens on Magrath Avenue. Like most castles of this date but in contrast to the earlier defences the strongest features were the gatehouse, which was to stand until 1842 (**28**), and the curtain walls, which were to be maintained until the end of the sixteenth century. Within the walls there stood the three-storey Great Hall, made for the king to stay in (although he only ever came for two nights, when he complained about the smell from the stables beneath his upper chamber) and a chapel. All these buildings were of stone, and more mundane structures such as a separate kitchen and stable block were added in the next century in cheaper materials. The functions of the old wooden castle otherwise continued much as before, however much the surroundings had improved. As a royal castle in the heart of England and away from the likelihood of invasion (though this was never seen as impossible), its main uses were administrative duties related to the shire. The sheriff, later the constable, lived and worked here, courts were held, treasure and official documents were kept (although the former might be left at Barnwell for greater security), and it was a prison equipped with stocks, a pillory and gallows.

Accounts of the fifteenth century show that the defences were still being repaired then, though at times they were in a poor state. The Great Hall was disused and roofless when Henry VI gave its stones to go towards the building of King's College, but all the military features appear to have been intact until the mid sixteenth century. In the reign of Elizabeth I, however, the constant expenses of repair in addition to a ready market for good quality stone for colleges, led to rapid destruction. It was stated in early seventeenth century depositions that 'the digging up of foundations and taking down was first done in the reign of Queen Mary by Sir John Huddlestone for re-edifying his house at Sawston'. Huddlestone had seen his old house burned after he gave shelter to Mary I before she was accepted as queen, but the main features of the castle still stood in 1585, with the keep described as being more imposing than Oxford's. At this time it was argued, probably with some exaggeration, that the castle was in ruins, and the queen gave permission for stone to be sold, most notably for Emmanuel and Magdalene Colleges and Great St. Mary's church. Before this permission had been given to tip rubbish into the ditch. Even so, Elizabeth still expected that the walls themselves must be kept in repair, so the defensive function of the site was not supposed to be ignored, and the administrative functions were important enough to require a new Jury House and a Shire Hall in 1572. But good building stone was now in huge demand in Cambridge and supplies from medieval monuments such as religious houses and castles were irresistible. When Frederick, Duke of Wurtemberg visited in 1592 he inspected 'the old ruined and decayed palace or castle...it has the appearance of having been formerly a very strong place of defence, but is now only used for keeping prisoners in some of the vaults'. By the beginning of 1606 there was an official survey from which W M Palmer deciphered these convincing descriptions of the castle's fate:

> There remaneth the gatehouse used as a common gaol and dwelling of the gaoler. All the rest of the walls of the castle and their foundations are razed and utterly ruinated saving a parcel of land on the NW side which has a convenient house builded unto it for the use of the Grand Jury and safe keeping of jurors that enquire and pass upon trials for the King and his people at the Assizes, Gaol deliveries and Sessions.

A View of Cambridge Castle from ẙ Hill

29   A view from Cambridge castle drawn by James Essex in 1740, showing a ditch around the
mound containing a gallows next to a clump of trees, the medieval gatehouse on the left hand
side, one of Cromwell's bastions, the three-storey Cromwellian barracks, and, on the far right,
the timber buildings of the Elizabethan law courts, or Shire Hall, which stood until 1747

> The site of the Castle, with yards, trenches, hills and void ground, some being
> pasture ground and some covered with rubbage and ruines of the Castle,
> containeth by estimation about 5 acres, and are worth, excepting Shire House,
> Jury House and gatehouse £6 8s 4d.

In 1609 the official record for Cambridge castle is 'decayed, but used by the Justices of the
Assize in theire circuits and for the County prisons'. (**29**)

Later records refer to the rent raised for the Crown by letting out grazing rights and
four cottages that had been put up in the now-dry castle ditch. These grazing rights were
jealously guarded, with shepherds watching to make sure animals from Chesterton did
not stray onto this pasture, and long court cases were fought out because it was not
resolved whether the land occupied by the castle had now reverted to the manor of
Chesterton. However the structure and functions of the castle were not at this time seen
as a royal problem. From the evidence given by long-lived witnesses during the various
cases that were heard we get a remarkable picture of a monument that temporarily lost all
purpose. For example, they remembered the moat only as the place where a cottage was
built for a poor tenant: 'a noisome, foul ditch, which was filled up by earth and gravel
digged up from the castle'. Water running under a wide stone arch over the ditch between
the gatehouse and the barbican and around the castle mound in living memory was *'where
Goode's house is now standing'*, and a rose garden surrounded by a round wall was created
where an old pond between the castle mound and St. Giles' church was filled with rubbish

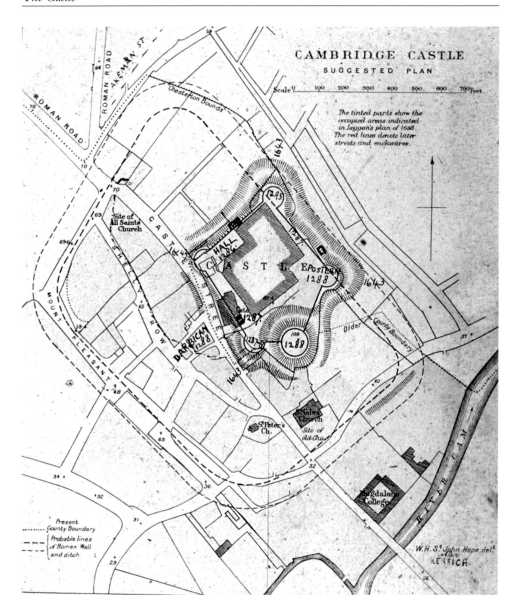

30   *Plan of Cambridge castle made in 1895*

31   A pastoral view from Cambridge Castle in 1841, drawn by John le Keux

left as the stonework on the mound was pulled down. Cottages mentioned in these disputes are shown in Le Keux's engraving, when the pastoral character of this part of the town was still very evident (**31**).

Up to this time the roles and history of Cambridge castle fit with the general pattern of royal castles that were not close to sensitive border regions, but in the tables of expenditure for all periods it seems to be the cheapest to run. In its first two centuries it only cost about 30s per year, and in 1287, for example, £5 was paid to the constable, about a quarter of the average, and a half of the next cheapest ones, a lowly figure that was maintained in later centuries. To some extent this perhaps reflects the hospitality available elsewhere for the king's visits.

It is ironic that only a few years after the quiet collapse and despoliation of a castle that had cost the Crown much effort to maintain and garrison for five centuries, it was at last seen as having real military worth during the Civil War, but on the rebel not the royal side. Oliver Cromwell was the local MP and had also studied at Cambridge. He made it the centre for the Eastern Association, and in 1642 it was reported in Parliament that 'Mr Cromwell had seized the Magazine at Cambridge.' Times were interesting in the town, for the university was in the main strongly Royalist, whilst the townspeople and the surrounding countryside mostly supported the Roundheads. The defence of Cambridge was seen as a priority early on in the War, and continued in rather a half-hearted fashion throughout. At first an army of 23,000 gathered here, but this was soon reduced to a garrison of 1000, and Cromwell sent out an apparently successful appeal through local churches to raise £2000 for new defences. In 1643 the Governor of Cambridge reported that 'our town and castle are now very strongly fortified being encompassed with Breast Works and Bulwarks', and the Jury House was converted for barracks. The fortifications were all earthworks, once again reusing and deepening the Roman ditch to the north-east and the medieval ditch around the motte, and building at least three triangular bastions to site cannons. The bridges in Cambridge were demolished at the same time, so the castle regained control of the river and its crossing point once more. For the archaeologist Cromwell's work was a disaster. His ditches were larger than any that preceded them, and all investigations of medieval and even, on the north side, of Roman defences, have revealed nothing but post-medieval materials.

Quite soon the other tradition of Cambridge castle was repeated; constant complaints about its neglect by the central powers. This time it was usually lack of money to pay or even feed the soldiers garrisoned here. One letter reads 'There is such want of arms we know not what to do. The soldiers demand coats, shoes and money ... I never saw worse tattered soldiers for the General'. Later complaints include 'The soldier is likely to starve, the inhabitants disinabled to relieve them, being undone by the burden of quarter yet unpaid'. At the same time there were official demands that they hold more adequate provisions so that they could withstand the Royalist attacks which were expected. In 1646, with the War almost finished, the order came for the defences to be demolished, the soldiers and horses be sent to Ireland, and that no 'horse, powder, arms or ammunition or other instruments of warre' be wasted or embezzled. This last phase of military occupation was now over.

Use of the site for administration and justice continued. In 1665 a local alderman and diarist Samuel Newton records at first hand how, at one Assize here, a robber suffered the horrible fate of being pressed to death — 'he was about an hour a dyeing' — because, in order to save his family's inheritance, he refused to plead guilty or not guilty. Another man was put in the pillory and two more were hanged, one for murdering his wife and the other for stealing a mare. At the same time, much of the castle area was used for very little apart from grazing. In 1669, for example, Newton mentions 'Alsoe was granted to Mr. Maior license to plant trees on the waste at the Castle end on the banke next to Mr. Storyes ground'. The high point of the motte was useful for national celebrations, and when a son was born to James II in 1688 'Great St. Mary's bells rang and a Bonfire was on the Great Hill in Cambridge and the souldiers there mett and gave severall volleys of shott'. In 1747 a new Shire Hall was built in the market place and the Elizabethan hall on Castle Hill was pulled down, but the gatehouse was used as a prison up to 1802. In that year the Castle ditch, in which the gallows had stood, was filled in as part of the exercise of lowering the whole Castle yard before a new prison was built. John Bowtell, one of Cambridge's early antiquarians, observed the removal of soil in 1802, and described many burials that were seen then, the wells and cellars of houses, animal bones, stone bullets and many artefacts from Cromwell's time; 'tobacco pipes of fine white clay ... were mingled with the martial spoils in this multifarious domain'. Shortly afterwards a new prison was made where the brick Cromwellian barracks, later used as a House of Correction and the Governor's residence, had stood. Then, in 1842, 'A new and handsome Shire House within the precincts of the castle was completed ... To the great regret of the lovers of antiquity, the spacious and massive Gatehouse, the sole relic of the Castle, was removed to make way for this Shire House'.

The prison was used until 1915, and the last execution took place in 1913. Some years after it closed it was intended to bring a branch of the Public Record Office here, for the site was still in the Crown's ownership. At this time the local historian WM Palmer described it as 'desolate, and worse than desolate, encumbered with an unwanted prison, mean tenements, bushes and rubbish'. Unfortunately for Cambridge the records were soon returned to London, for Cambridgeshire County Council acquired the site and Shire Hall was built in 1931/2, using materials from the demolished County Gaol. For many years the area was shared with streets of Victorian houses, but in the post-War planning boom temporary buildings and car parks for increasing numbers of County Council officers took their place, particularly when, in 1974, local government reorganisation brought Cambridgeshire and Huntingdonshire into one jurisdiction. This unravelled the administrative pattern of a millennium but in one way was reminiscent of the old Saxon earls and Norman sheriffs who had also ruled both counties from this site. One new office block, the Octagon, designed to fit into the shape and character of one of Cromwell's bastions, went up in 1974, and much of the remaining site was redeveloped with office blocks for the County Council and commercial users in the early 1980s (**colour plate 4**). Nuclear bunkers even maintain the defensive theme of the castle.

Continuity of land-use, led by the needs for authority and military security to exist together in a central place with good communications, separate from the area of commerce and settlement, has long been characteristic of Castle Hill. Sadly, this is not reflected in survivals on the ground. The motte, without its ditch and somewhat altered in shape by Elizabethan stone robbers, Cromwell's soldiers and twentieth-century needs to give safe access to many thousands of visitors a year, is still a magnificent view-point (**colour plate 5**), and the disturbed remains of two Civil War bastions can be found. Otherwise, it is only the steep fall in the land to the north-west and the cracks in houses that ignored the ditches beneath them, that remind us what once stood.

5 Medieval religious houses
in the town

Monasteries, priories, friaries, hospitals and other religious houses were important features of most medieval towns, but what makes Cambridge unusual is the number of friars who came to study rather than to preach. It was the humble houses for scholar-monks, the Dominicans, Franciscans, Austin friars, Carmelites and Friars of the Sack, which had lasting influences over the town, both by their eager use of academic facilities and interaction with the infant university, and by their accumulation of inner-city properties that could be adapted to later colleges.

The first and largest religious house in Cambridge, however, was Barnwell Priory, which never became involved in university life. It was one of the earliest Augustinian houses of Regular Canons in Britain, originally intended to house and support a group of six priests to serve neighbouring churches. These Augustinian, or Austin, canons were monks who followed a looser rule than the orders that were confined to their cloisters. They were expected to work in the community, 'preaching, baptizing and reconciling penitents' in the words of the pope in 1116. They were often located in or near towns where they might serve as parish priests and also work in health, education, singing masses for the dead and distributing poor relief. Their financial support partly came from the tithes of parish churches rather than the agricultural estates that the Benedictines, in particular, accumulated. In Cambridge, their house was first founded by sheriff Picot in 1092, on or close to St. Giles' church, near to his castle. This benefaction was allegedly in fulfilment of a vow made for the recovery of his wife from a dangerous illness. However there were also good and economical reasons for having his own foundation, eligible to collect extensive tithes and commanding the route between the river and castle, especially if, as seems probable, he was taking over an existing Saxon minster.

After Picot's death and the flight overseas of his son following a failed rebellion, the house of canons was apparently deserted. Pain Peverel, the Norman knight who succeeded to Picot's holdings, gained the king's permission to refound it on a more pleasant and spacious site on common land within the royal manor of Chesterton, thus freeing a valuable town-site for his own possession. This new site was on the north-eastern outskirts of Cambridge, where a holy well marked a religious site with pre-Christian origins that was used for semi-pagan festivities in Saxon times. A hermit had also lived here, in 'a tiny wooden oratory'. Relics brought back from the Crusades by Peverel and the proceeds from several village churches were given to support the Priory, and there were private donations by townspeople over the years, usually of strips of land within the open fields. Other major benefactors included King John, who granted it the manor of Chesterton for a favourable price. Another source of income that was to be increasingly important was the grant of proceeds from Midsummer Fair which, given its obvious pagan origins, must have been flourishing long before a royal grant was given or the monks arrived.

Building on a lavish scale was always a feature of Barnwell Priory. A new church was dedicated in 1170, and in the early thirteenth century a refectory, guest hall, infirmary, granary, stables, bakehouse, brewhouse, gatehouse and two chapels were added to what was already a substantial complex. The practical nature of some of these structures illustrates the importance of professional management to this large agricultural holding. In fact, too much concern with efficiency brought the monks into conflict with townspeople on more than one occasion, particularly because the common land on which they were sited included a droveway to the river, and restrictions on the use of this were much resented. Arguments over common rights, and especially attempts to enclose parcels of land and to plant trees led directly to attacks during the Peasants Revolt in 1381. Walls were broken down, trees felled and stores stolen. Similar disputes continued in the fifteenth century, when tenants refused their customary services.

The number of monks at Barnwell was quite small, the seventeen taxed in 1379 probably being one of the highest totals, and they were generally outnumbered by their servants. Their functions were the traditional ones of hospitality, charity, education, learning and prayer, as well as acting as parish priests. They certainly must have offered comfortable quarters to their guests, for Barnwell was almost always chosen by royalty when visits were made to Cambridge, and it was a matter of comment when Edward I resided for a night at the castle he had just repaired at great expense. He too returned to Barnwell on his next visit. On the one occasion Parliament met in Cambridge, the whole court lodged here. It is not known how far down the social scale such hospitality extended, but it was normal for travellers of many sorts to use religious houses. A boys' school was attached to the Priory, supported by gifts of charity, and the collections of books in the library suggests that the monks themselves spent much time in study, transcribing texts and compiling their own chronicles. There was an infirmary for sick and aged monks, but no record that this served a wider purpose. Five poor men were supported at the Priory, and scraps were used to feed three other poor people every day, plus general gifts of peas and beans to townspeople in Lent.

The small number of monks and squabbles over elections of a new prior laid Barnwell open to the early attentions of Thomas Cromwell, and the house was dissolved in 1538. It was too far out of town to be taken over for a new college, and no one was interested in the estate as a going concern. After the church furnishings were sold and the roofs stripped, the walls were left to become a quarry for building stone, some of it being taken for the new chapel of Corpus Christi. Some of the ruins were still standing in the early nineteenth century when they were drawn by Richard Relhan (**colour plate 6**), but were dug away shortly afterwards, leaving little trace. One part that survives is the small, square building known as the Cellarers Chequer, in Abbey Road (**colour plate 7**). This is a single-vaulted chamber, built between 1213 and 1265, and was probably a kitchen. It now contains three stone coffins and various architectural fragments of twelfth- and thirteenth- century date. Parts of the old boundary wall of Abbey House are likely to have been part of the priory walls, and there are many carved fragments from the priory in the gardens of Abbey House. The Abbey Church, built for parishioners well away from the monks' area of worship, is still in use.

The next religious house founded in Cambridge, the Benedictine nunnery of St Radegund's, was a more humble institution, as women's houses generally were. Its location just outside the bounds of the medieval town, however, meant that its premises and estates were valuable properties which were converted into Jesus College in 1496, and as such its altered form has survived. A nunnery was in existence early in the twelfth century, when it started to accumulate gifts of small parcels of land. Later in that century it was given land on or adjacent to Grenecroft, now Midsummer Common, a spacious site where country meadows butted up against the town. Like Barnwell, the number of religious inhabitants was small, about twelve at maximum. Fifteenth-century accounts show that the nunnery was running a large farming estate together with various related business activities (for example, wool from their own sheep was woven and dyed on site). There was an annual market in the adjacent Garlic Lane (now Park Street), and to judge by the purchases of food, drink and table linen for the guest-hall, the nuns were providing considerable hospitality. The scale and quality of the surviving portions of their church also show that wealth was not lacking. Both the nuns' accounts and the archaeological discoveries of recent years point to a good and plentiful but not luxurious diet, in contrast to evidence for a richer diet indicated by animal bones derived from their successors — the fellows of Jesus College. In both collections there are the bones of cattle, sheep, pig and horse, showing that mutton and beef were staples. However, whereas the nuns' refuse contained only small percentages of chicken, goose and fish bones, that of the fellows was also notable for game such as red deer, hare, rabbit, mallard, wood pigeon and a wide variety of fish.

In 1487 Bishop Alcock declared that the nuns were unfit to elect their own prioress in the usual way, and so made his own appointment and other decisions. A few years later the number of nuns had been reduced to two and he was able to declare that 'the carelessness, improvidence, and dissolute conduct of the prioress and nuns', had led to 'such want and poverty that they are unable in any way to perform Divine Service, or their accustomed duties, whether of religion, mercy or hospitality', and he was consequently free to take over their properties in order to found a college. This should not be taken too seriously; his complaints were virtually word for word the same as the reasons given for abolishing other charities at this time, such as St John's hospital, and are not necessarily a fair picture of the nuns' failures. In particular, there does not seem to have been extra money found for the future support of fellows and students at the college beyond the rents and other incomes the nuns had built up, and no evidence for changes in the management of the estate (**32**).

One surviving glory of this nunnery is the church, dating to the twelfth and thirteenth centuries, whose chancel is still used by the college as its chapel. It has lost its aisles, side-chapels and much of its nave, but is still a large building. Outside it can be seen parts of a medieval doorway and windows, remains of a prioress's tomb, and a bench where the feet

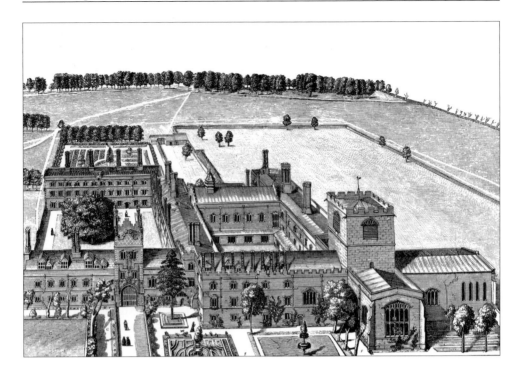

32   Jesus College, still dominated by the nuns' church, drawn by Loggan in 1688

of the poor were washed on Maundy Thursday. Recent examination of college fabric during extensive repair works has shown that the masonry of the chapter house was incorporated into the east range of Cloister Court (**33**) where a handsome thirteenth-century doorway stands, but generally the medieval buildings have not survived. Even so, it is noticeable that that these despised nuns were the only religious house to leave significant surviving structural remains. Their site too, in the forefront of classic Cambridge 'country in the town' tradition and still separated by the running water of Jesus Brook on one side, is a worthy reminder of their presence here (**colour plate 8**) .

Intellectual life did not impinge on the lives of the nuns of St Radegund's, despite Bishop Alcock's insinuations about the deleterious effect of the university on their behaviour. The Benedictines of Barnwell also appear to have exhibited no interest in formal education, even preferring to pay fines rather than send any member of their house to a university despite the convenience of having one so close. The new religious orders of Franciscans and Dominicans who began arriving in the thirteenth century, though, had quite different aspirations and organisations, and their presence was to have far more influence on the development of the university and the future role of the town.

These were mendicant orders, supposedly holding no property but dependant on day-to-day charity. Their dense concentration and their lives of study in Cambridge eventually made this impracticable here, and special houses were built by them. It was the intellectual

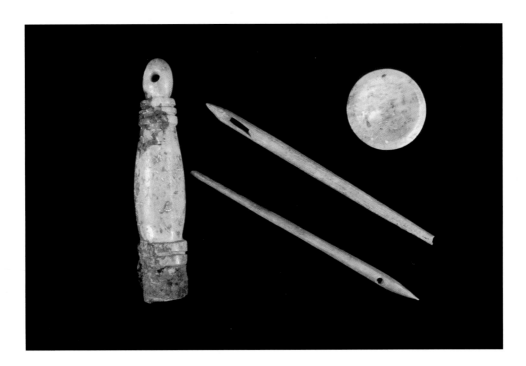

1   *Bone objects, found near to where they were probably made on Castle Hill*

2   *An oculist's stamp, used for labelling eye ointment, found on Castle Hill.*
      Photograph: copyright Cambridge University Museum of Archaeology and Anthropology.

3   Stone carving from Arbury

4   Cambridge Castle in 1800, with the tower of St Peter's.
     Drawn by Richard Relhan

5   *An aerial view of St Giles' church and Cambridge Castle in 1988, with the modern buildings of Shire Hall and Castle Court beyond. Photograph: Geoffrey Robinson*

6   *The ruins of Barnwell Priory in the early nineteenth century, with the spire of Chesterton church in the background (extreme right), drawn by Richard Relhan.*

7   *The only surviving building of Barnwell Priory, the Cellarers Chequer in Abbey Road, drawn by Richard Relhan*

8   *Jesus College from across Jesus Brook, which separated the nunnery from Grenecroft, engraved by W Westall in 1815*

9 *Excavating fragments of the Austin Friary beneath the Cavendish Laboratory in Free School Lane*

10 *The twelfth-century chapel of the Leper Hospital, drawn by Richard Relhan in the early nineteenth century*

11   A section through the King's Ditch, exposed in 1970 when the Lion Yard car park was being constructed. Photograph: Ken Joysey.

12 (left)   Roman intaglio or ring setting, engraved with the god Bacchus
13 (right)   Sgraffito ware jug from Cambridge. Photograph: copyright, Cambridge University Museum of Archaeology and Anthropology

14   *Two medieval jugs from Cambridge. The left hand sherd, decorated with knights on horse back, was exported by sea via King's Lynn from Scarborough where its production was promoted by Cistercian monks. The thirteenth-century jug on the right is from Brill, Northamptonshire. Photograph: Cambridge University Museum of Archaeology and Anthropology*

15   *Excavations under an extension to Trinity library in 1990, uncovering waterlogged remains of twelth-century buildings*

16 *Excavations of the Provost's Lodge, with Great St Mary's church and the sixteenth-century buildings of King's Parade in the background*

17 *Ornamentation on Christ's gatehouse, resplendent with the insignia of Lady Margaret Beaufort and the Tudor family*

19   *The screen built by Wilkins to finish the courtyard at King's College*

20   *Trinity Great Court, engraved by W Westall in 1815. King Edward's tower is on the far left, the Elizabethan chapel is in the background and the fountain, using water from the Francisian's conduit and built not long afterwards in classical style, in front. Henry VIII's great gate is on the right, flanked by medieval remains of King's Hall. This view is similar today*

21   *Pembroke College and chapel, said to be the view from the poet Thomas Gray's window in Peterhouse. The waters of Hobson's Conduit can be seen running along either side of the road. Old buildings on the left have been replaced with the Emmanuel Congregational church. Engraved by F Mackenzie in 1815*

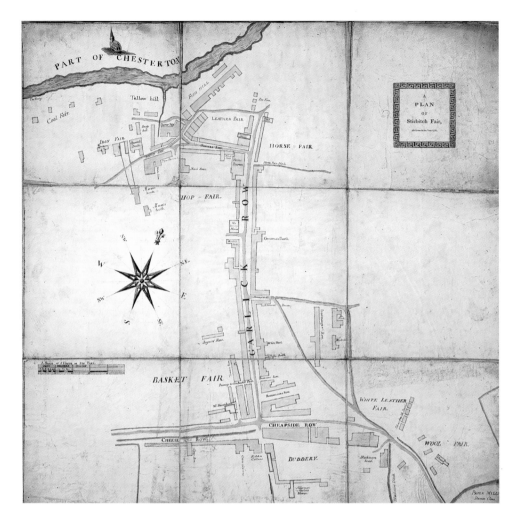

22   *A map of Sturbridge Fair made by James Tall in 1816, copying from a 1775 copy of a plan made in 1726*

23 *St Luke's in New
    Chesterton, built in 1878
    for the growing suburban
    population and designed,
    very typically at this time,
    like a medieval village
    church*

24 *A view of Cherry Hinton in the early nineteenth century, seen from the hills to the south-west.
    Drawn by Richard Relhan*

25 *The Cam from Magdalene Bridge today*

26 *Barges being towed by a horse along the back of Clare college. Engraved by Augustus Pugin in 1815.*

27   *A gasometer near the Cambridge Museum of Technology in Cheddars Lane*

28   *Cattle grazing on the Backs near King's College*

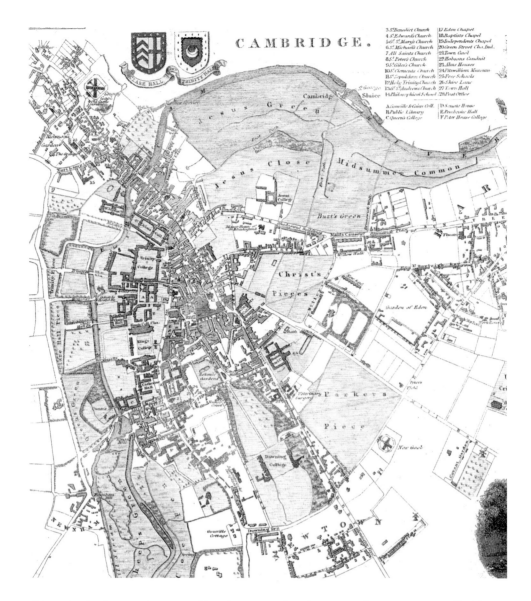

29   *Cambridge in 1837, mapped by Thomas Moule. There is new housing in Barnwell and New Town, but otherwise the rural setting is intact*

30 *Cambridge market from the tower of Great St Mary's. The row of shops behind includes sixteenth and seventeenth century buildings, and not far in the distance are the open spaces of Midsummer Common and beyond*

31 *Emmanuel Congregational church, seen from Little St Mary's churchyard*

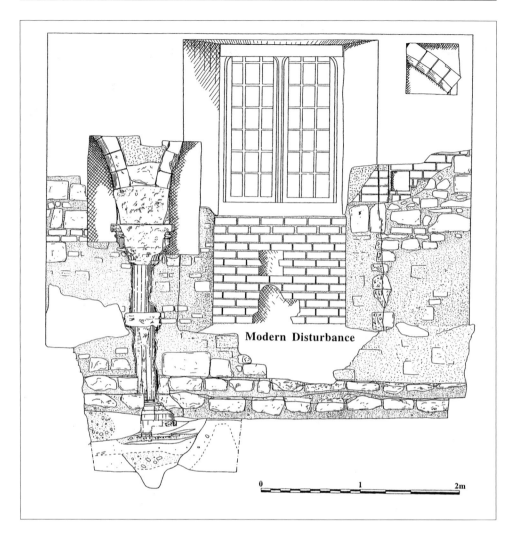

Modern Disturbance

33   *Medieval masonry of the nuns' chapter house, recorded by Cambridge Archaeology Unit when plaster was removed in Jesus College*

life, stimulated by the need to understand and defend orthodox theology and the revival of preaching in place of the traditional monastic life, that brought them to Cambridge, as to Oxford, in great numbers. They came because teaching was available but once here they were to have decisive influences on the medieval development of the university. Monkish traditions of communal life, academic dress, use of Latin and many other aspects of college life derive from these early student-friars, and the steady demand for more and more educational facilities gave constant impetus for the survival and growth of the university itself.

The Franciscan friars, inspired by the life and example of St Francis of Assisi to live in poverty and save the souls of the poor by preaching, arrived in England in 1224 and within a few weeks had set up houses in London, Northampton, Oxford and Cambridge. It was necessary to their mission to live in or close to towns, but the choice of the capital plus the three towns where student life was beginning was no coincidence. They recognised that it was necessary to ensure intellectual rigour and credibility before their message spread more widely, and this in itself is an interesting comment on the very early days of the university. They were joined in Cambridge by the Dominicans, who had come to England in 1221. They were the first order for whom intellectual discipline, to be used in defence of the established church against heretical ideas that were already seen as a threat in St Dominic's homeland in southern Spain, was the main purpose. To this end they sought out learned novices and gave them a long period of training together with close contact with university life. Their brethren at all levels moved easily between the universities of Europe, another tradition they have passed to modern academics, and they were thus very much part of the way in which ideas spread and developed at that time.

In 1226 the first Franciscans in Cambridge were lent a disused synagogue adjoining the gaol on the site of the present Guildhall. Four brothers built an 'exceedingly humble' chapel here, uncomfortably sharing an entrance with the gaolers until they were able to expand over an adjoining lane and two house plots. Cambridge was a centre for this Order, with about sixty of the brothers studying here. Appreciation of the contribution of the Cambridge brothers to education was shown by regular gifts by successive kings, still continuing in the sixteenth century. Later they moved to a site that is now Sidney Sussex (**34**), and in 1350 a new church, large enough to be regularly used for university ceremonies and with an adjacent cemetery and cloister, was dedicated. In order to have a safe water supply the monks built a conduit to their house from springs near the Cambridge Observatory. At the dissolution this conduit was given to Trinity College, and still feeds the fountain in Great Court. Together with the Dominicans, the Franciscans were closely involved with the foundation of a Theology Faculty in the mid thirteenth century. This lead to endless squabbles over the monks right to study theology without taking a lengthy Arts course first, even without which between ten and fifteen years of study were normal.

The friars were well aware of Henry VIII's intentions in 1538 and they had left with all their valuable books, and no doubt any other important items, before his men arrived. The university attempted in vain to keep the church for its own use, but the buildings were demolished and 3000 loads of stone from here went towards the building of Trinity's chapel. Sidney Sussex was not founded until 1596, by which time most of the damage had been done. One building survived to 1776 and was used as the college chapel. William Cole records how this 'was pulled entirely downe, with some new Buildings erected by it by D. Paris, the late Master.' Their architect was James Essex, who made a ground plan of the old building in relation to the new, as well as describing the remains. He even included some archaeological comments about 'the quantity of small bones of fowl, rabbits and other animals, with spoons etc', from which he concludes the building was a refectory, though a kitchen is more likely. Nothing now remains of the Franciscan buildings, but an excavation trench and resistivity surveys show that the friary church was in Cloister Court, where a major masonry building with window glass and burials were found, and that Hall Court was laid out to the same plan as the original cloister with the medieval buildings beneath the existing ones.

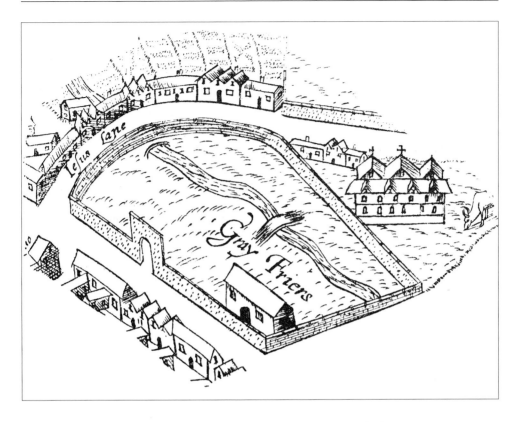

34   The site the Franciscan friary in 1574, before Sidney Sussex was built

The Dominicans, or Black Friars, were probably even more important than the Franciscans in intellectual developments at Cambridge, although their dogma sometimes put them at odds with university authorities and their principal remit, the counteraction of all possible heresies, seems a strange combination with scholasticism. They were becoming established in the town in 1238, when the king gave them oak trees to build a church on a site just outside the Barnwell Gate, where Emmanuel College now stands. The house continued to grow and flourish in later centuries, receiving royal support and many privileges for the monks, always more than fifty in number, who studied here. Like the Franciscans, the Dominicans left England before their house had to surrender to the king. They must have managed to rescue some of their library for a few of their books are in Rome, but most of it was lost or destroyed. The friary, with its 'barns, stables, dovehouses, orchards, gardens, ponds, stews, waters, land' etc, as described in 1583, was leased out, but the buildings were pulled down, stone and timber going to Great St Mary's. When Emmanuel College was founded in 1594 it was strictly Puritan, so every trace of the monks' church was supposed to be removed, although the church and part of the claustral range do appear on Loggan's drawing of 1688. Hidden traces survive in the hall and Combination Room, where thirteenth-century windows and medieval fireplaces were found behind panelling. There is one medieval buttress in New Court and other elements are being discovered as opportunities arise to record and excavate during building works. In 1993, for example, remains of a previously unknown North Building were excavated, a luxurious stone structure of the late fourteenth century that had floors of decorative glazed tiles and painted glass in the windows. The excavator, Alison Dickens, suggests this building may have been a guest house for those attending the only Parliament that met in Cambridge, held in this priory in 1388. The gateway that was in front of Emmanuel was standing in the eighteenth century, for William Cole took stones from there to stand by his front door at Milton.

Several other religious orders were attracted to Cambridge during the middle ages. These include the Carmelites, yet another mendicant order, which had begun as groups of monks living as hermits in Palestine, some of whom were brought to England by Crusaders in the thirteenth century. They first had a house in Chesterton but afterwards built a church and monastic buildings in Newnham, isolated in a patch of fenland and a strange home after the desert. A few members of the order objected to this move and stayed in Chesterton, taking the name 'Brethren of Blessed Mary'. Later, this breakaway group seems to have moved closer into Cambridge, and built a church within the parish of All Saints by the Castle, to which Barnwell Priory made strong objection. No trace of them has been found after the mid fourteenth century.

The Newnham site was suitable for seclusion and peaceful contemplation in ascetic conditions, but not for travelling to lectures in the winter. Having already become involved in teaching and study, the Carmelites at Newnham officially changed from a contemplative to a preaching order. Despite the objections of other religious orders they moved to Milne Street in central Cambridge at the end of the thirteenth century, pulling down ordinary houses between the road and the river to make space for their own buildings. They were therefore the first order to take over a development site in the area that the university was to make its own. Over the next few years they were able to enlarge and enclose their site, stopping and building over lanes as they did so. In particular, they were allowed to enclose their property with two walls down to the river, provided gates were left in them so townsmen could reach the river if this was necessary for defence. During excavations when a new building was being added to Queens' College some of the monks' burials were found, and also clunch footings, thought to be part of the conventual buildings, that went down to a depth of 17ft. One of the Friary's functions was to act as a treasury, guarding university deeds and valuables, and it was presumably for this role that the wrath of the townsmen led to a violent raid on their church during the Peasants Revolt. Several of the Carmelites in Cambridge achieved high academic distinctions and were involved in various acrimonious exchanges with their rivals, the Dominicans,

By the late fifteenth century successive heads of these Carmelites had interests elsewhere, and the life of the order declined. In 1538, Queens' College, holder of the adjoining site, claimed there were only two members of the community left (which in this case seems to have been correct) and so asked for it to be dissolved and its site and property be passed to them. All of the extensive group of buildings were soon demolished. Part of the north wall of the church, containing a fourteenth-century doorway, survives in the Fellows' Garden at Queens', and stained glass roundels now reused in the college library show the heads of Carmelite friars (**35**).

35   The head of a Carmelite monk depicted on a roundel in Queens' College library

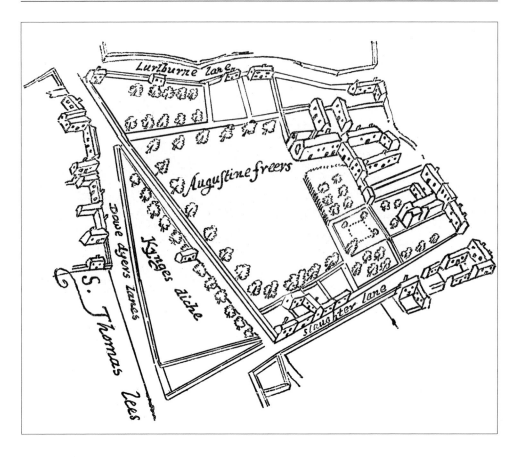

36   The site of the Austin friars house in 1592. Dowe dyers Lanes *is Downing Street, and*
Slaughter Lane *is Corn Exchange Street*

Another rule that had begun as groups of hermits was the Austin Friars. They were
given a small piece of land near St Benet's Street at the end of the thirteenth century,
extending this to include a large area of the town that is now mostly the New Museums
site, between Downing Street, Free School Lane and Corn Exchange Street (**36**). Two
walls running down to the King's Ditch enclosed their site. They came to Cambridge for
educational rather than religious reasons, and were a lively and troublesome order that was
involved in both town and university politics. Their position in the town-centre also led
to property disputes and quarrels with more established orders, especially Barnwell Priory.
Intellectually, they were free-thinkers, in contrast to the Dominicans in particular, and
were in contact with the Reform movement in Germany where the Austin Friars were
early supporters of Luther. Most of the scholars who met at the White Horse Inn close to
the Friary, and who were nick-named 'Little Germany', were Austin Friars. One of their
members in this Cambridge house was Robert Barnes, who was burned as a heretic in
1540, and another was Miles Coverdale, translator of the Bible into English and a leading
reformer in Elizabeth's reign.

The Refectory of St Augustins Monastery Cambridge —
1780.

37   An eighteenth-century sketch of the last surviving fragment of the Austin Friary

This order seems to have abolished itself, unsurprisingly in view of its religious politics, in the 1530s. Its buildings were quarried away, though one building, probably the infirmary or guest hall remained before it was demolished in the 1790s. It was lived in by Thomas Buck, the university printer, and an eighteenth-century view of it from a window in Corpus Christi shows it with later fashions in windows inserted (**37**). Remains of buildings and the cemetery have been excavated during building works, most recently beneath the Cavendish Laboratory in Free School Lane, where walls and floors were found and preserved (**colour plate 9**). Other architectural fragments, including doorways and part of a fourteenth-century arch have been reset in the basement of the Scientific Periodicals library.

Two other small groups of monks who settled in Cambridge specifically to study were the Friars of the Sack, apparently protégés of Barnwell who gave them a stone house with its own chapel on Trumpington Street, on the site that is now the Fitzwilliam Museum. They were only there for about fifty years, as minor orders of this kind were then banned. On the opposite side of the road, on the site of Old Addenbrooke's hospital (now the Judge Institute), another redundant private chapel was given to the Gilbertine order of Sempringham, Norfolk, in 1291, to be a centre of learning for all its houses. It remained here until 1539. Both these houses were effectively colleges of students and must have seemed virtually indistinguishable from the first secular college, their neighbour Peterhouse, which only just preceded them. The same applies to Buckingham college, created in 1428 by Crowland Abbey for their monks and other Benedictines living and studying in Cambridge, which was taken over as Magdalene College in 1542.

Caring for the sick was another religious duty, though it was taken less seriously than scholastic pursuits in Cambridge. The principal hospital, that of St John, was to have a lasting impression on both the town and university of Cambridge for it colonised another area by the river, preparing the site for one of the great Cambridge colleges. The land used was a patch of marshy waste previously used as commons by the townspeople, and was therefore conveniently available. But the hospital also served as a money-lending institution, and its creation within the Jewry was presumably to make the point that Christian merchants should look after each other. It was founded in about 1200 and received generous endowments from many townspeople, especially the Dunning family whose stone-built manor house, known as the School of Pythagoras, still stands in the grounds of St John's College. Its functions were to care for the sick, except pregnant women, lepers, the wounded, paralysed cripples and the insane, who were supposed to go to St Radegund's, the Leper hospital and St Anthony's. The poor were given food and clothes on St John's Day. There were also lodgers on various bases of payment and charity. Quite early on it was drawn into university life, for Hugh de Balsham, bishop of Ely, used it to provide hostel accommodation for his monks, *'studious scholars'* from Ely, when they were at Cambridge. The mixture of students and invalids was perhaps not such a good idea, so in 1284 the bishop took what was later seen as a momentous step, sending the scholars to hostels on Trumpington Street, the origin of Peterhouse.

St John's hospital continued to provide valuable services for the sick, but by about 1500 was said to be in decline, identical complaints being made as those against St Radegund's at the same time. Lady Margaret, mother of Henry VII, gained the bishop's permission to convert it into a college. The valuable site, with its buildings and numerous endowments given throughout the medieval period, were handed over in 1511. Its chapel alone survived until 1868, when it was decided to pull down the medieval building and replace it with the tasteless Victorian structure that stands there now. Drawings made during this phase of destruction give some idea of the quality of stonework used (**38**). In order to bring this stone to the site a small canal was built from the river. This was discovered during excavations for the new library extension, and was shown to have been in use to the end of the fifteenth century, presumably being infilled when the hospital was converted to a college.

The early twelfth-century church of the leper hospital on Newmarket Road, another of Cambridge's early hospitals, fortunately does survive thanks to its remote position and also its usefulness as a chapel for Barnwell and later as a store-shed for Sturbridge Fair. This hospital was built well outside the town, the customary site used for lepers, which would have included those with syphilis and other venereal diseases, especially those causing disfigurement. These problems were thought to be linked with sexual sin, causing both extra horror to the medieval population and also especial reasons for prominent shows of charity to the penitent. Such hospitals were therefore built outside settlements, but not in isolated or discreet areas. Instead, it was common to find them on conspicuous sites by the highways near the entrances to towns, where passers-by would benefit from this exhibition of divine justice and admire the piety of their benefactors. Houses and

38   Remains of the medieval chapel of St John's hospital, demolished in 1863

other buildings for the patients were grouped around the church, whose present position, in a meadow next to a busy thoroughfare, is a striking continuation of this tradition. Such hospitals were also seen as an hygienic precaution by burgesses of the towns at a time when exotic diseases were one by-product of the Crusades. Although founded and endowed by townspeople it was taken over by the bishops of Ely, and in the late thirteenth century it ceased to look after the sick and became the chapel of St. Mary Magdalene, serving the population of Barnwell. It later stopped being used for religious purposes but was kept as a barn and store for traders at Sturbridge Fair. From here food was served while the fair was in progress, with stalls set up in the chapel yard. In the nineteenth century it was restored and used for a short time by labourers building the railway, and became the chapel for the Barnwell Military Hospital (**colour plate 10**). Architecturally, the Leper Chapel is important because its simple two-cell structure with very small round-headed windows and dog-tooth ornamented doors and arch is a complete and little altered example of a Norman church. Historically, the most significant event in the hospital's life was the grant enabling it to raise funds by holding an annual market and fair, for Sturbridge Fair was to grow into one of the greatest fairs in all Europe, vastly outgrowing its original owners

In the mid fourteenth century there was thought to be a need for another leper hospital, presumably because the first was being used for other purposes. One was founded by private donation, again on a highway outside the town, this time outside the Trumpington Gate at the corner of the Trumpington and Lensfield roads. It was known as the hospital of St Anthony and St Eloy (or Eligius), and still had a well-appointed chapel in the mid-sixteenth century, when it was referred to as the Spital House. It existed in a small way in the late seventeenth century, when it had been 'built up with brick within the memory of man in the room of a few old wooden cottages', where the poor were economically supported by begging, and the proceeds of an adjoining alehouse. The house was pulled down in 1852 and replaced with almshouses in Panton Street.

Differences in the futures of the institutions that arose from medieval piety and charity are due to events in the sixteenth century, when the powers of the monarchs and those close to them were so great that more traditional values, like the old faith, could be disregarded to an extraordinary degree. At this time, conversion of endowments from religious to educational functions benefited the souls and reputations of founders at minimum expense, and any survival of medieval fabric was an accidental by-product.

6 Development of the medieval town

Historical outline

At the end of the eleventh century most of the inhabitants of Cambridge were still primarily engaged in agriculture although they also had access to wealth and employment from trade and the administrative functions of a county town. Numerous churches and the Priory at Barnwell were either built or under construction, the castle in neighbouring Chesterton concentrated the king's mind on the town, and a local oligarchy of burgesses were in a position to control most developments. Later known as 'freemen', they were constrained only by the common rights that protected the agricultural interests of humbler inhabitants. Financially, in 1086 the town was valued at about ten times as much as the average village in this area and had a little more than ten times the population. Nationally it was only the fourteenth most significant borough, comparable to Huntingdon, for example, but it was situated in an economically buoyant area, for East Anglia and southern Cambridgeshire became the most densely settled and agriculturally wealthy part of Britain in the early middle ages, and its location made it accessible by land or water to most parts of the kingdom and to Europe. On the other hand, it was not on the sort of border or highway that would bring too much regular disruption in the medieval period, though proximity to the troublesome Fens brought dangers enough in the eleventh, twelfth and again in the thirteenth centuries.

In 1070 it was fortunate for the town that William made his base at Cambridge castle, while Hereward the Wake held the Isle of Ely and was free to raid Peterborough, looting and burning its cathedral amongst other damage. In 1088 however, the town was burned by Robert of Normandy, part of a campaign against his brother William Rufus. During the Anarchy period of the mid twelfth century Cambridge was sacked and burned by Geoffrey de Mandeville, with apparently no retaliation or offers of protection from forces in the castle. King John also arranged for strengthened defences and was himself sometimes in Cambridge during his own conflicts with powerful barons, but still the town was raided and the castle occupied by Prince Louis of France and the English rebels. This was in spite of expenditure on both the castle and other defences of the town ordered by John under his normally efficient commander, Fawkes de Bréauté. The last time Cambridge was caught up in the warfare of the middle ages was once again due to the ease with which Ely could be held by troublemakers. This time it was the barons known as the Disinherited, supporters of Simon de Montfort, who terrorised the town and raided villages such as Trumpington from the safety of the Isle. It seems that the principal sufferers were the Jews who were bringing prosperity to Cambridge with their trading contacts and capital, for the sad note in the Barnwell Chronicles for 1266 baldly states 'the Jews were killed'. The prior of Barnwell also made bitter complaints, and it was his monks who chronicled the

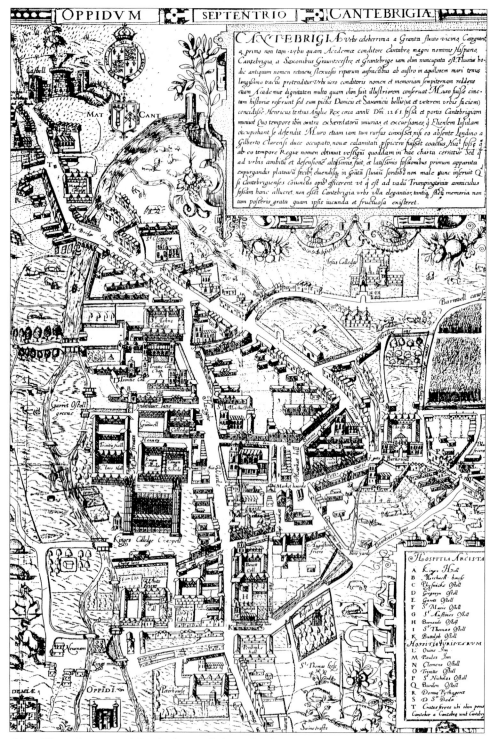

39   The earliest map of Cambridge, made by Richard Lyne in 1574. This shows the King's
      Ditch as the town boundary, with sheep, cattle and pigs grazing outside it

problems of this time, though the worst he really seems to have suffered was having to feed and house the soldiers and lose his horses to them.

As a result of the damage that was so easily inflicted, Henry III made serious attempts to provide Cambridge with a proper defensive system. It is interesting to note that he had no expectations of the royal castle providing any real protection for the townspeople on the other side of the river. William's fortification was *against* the town, not for it. In fact, Henry's defences proved equally useless, but at least they were in the right place, for he saw that the Saxon King's Ditch was sited to encircle most of the now built-up area, and so 'he caused gates to be made and ditches to be dug around the town with great diligence'. Some buildings had to be taken down for these constructions, so the work must have involved far more than just cleaning an old ditch, but the nature of the town in the late Saxon period makes it inconceivable that something on similar lines was not already in place. Henry had to withdraw his forces when he heard that London itself was at risk, whereupon the gates and other buildings were promptly burnt by the rebels. They were subsequently rebuilt, remaining a significant part of the town's geography throughout the middle ages, appearing on maps made in later years (**39**). Only one post of Barnwell Gate was still visible in 1573, when it was seen by Dr Caius. The origins and history of the King's Ditch still need some decisive archaeological work, single trenches through it being inevitably inconclusive as so much later scouring has destroyed its stratigraphy (**colour plate 11**). A dichotomy between its intended function and how it was actually used also causes confusion. There is no doubt that it was thought of as a military structure, with orders given for an 8ft-wide walkway to be left around it for easy manning, regular instructions to renew it at times of trouble, and provisions always made for access for defenders of the town when structures such as walls around religious houses were built. However, there is no record of anyone even trying to defend Cambridge by its means, whereas it functioned well as a customs barrier, with access limited to the Barnwell and Trumpington gates, and much of its route was the limit to settlement. Less satisfactorily, it was used as a water supply, even though it was also an open sewer and rubbish tip for several hundred years. McKenny Hughes noted the King's Ditch during construction of the Chemistry Laboratory in 1892 and described it as 'a single deep trench, which was filled with black silt and pottery and bones of medieval date', and similar rather unsatisfactory information was all that was obtained by much larger scale work in the 1970s.

The next period of unrest and fighting was a different kind of rebellion, known as the Peasants Revolt although the leading protagonists belonged to the minor gentry. Its progress in Cambridge was amongst the most bitter found anywhere, for there were innumerable disputes involving the interests of the university, townspeople, Barnwell Priory, government officials, and major and minor landowners. Some of this complexity is illustrated by the fact that it was the mayor, a representative of landowning interests and law and order, who led the mob in their attack on Barnwell Priory, and it was the town burgesses who were bound over not to obstruct the king's peace. It is interesting to note the divisions between those who led and those who suffered from this revolt, for it certainly had little to do with a starving peasantry against a landowning class. As so often in Cambridge, the division was not between town and country but ran across the interests

40   *Holy Trinity, engraved by John le Keux in 1841. The oldest remains in this church are
thirteenth century, but the first reference to it is in 1174, when it burned down*

of both. Ringleaders in the revolt included John Hanchach, holder of a manor in Shudy
Camps, and men of a similar class from the town, and their attacks were on anyone seen
as having official power. Apart from Barnwell Priory, damage was done to the property of
Roger Harleston, his manor houses in both Cambridge and the country being burnt, and
to the Franciscan friary. Documents of Corpus Christi College and those in the keeping
of the Carmelites were burnt, the contents of the muniments chest in Great St Mary's
church were destroyed, and there was a bonfire of official records in the market place.
Opportunities were taken to loot some valuables and to settle old scores, but the work of
the three days (which were all this trouble lasted) had specific aims. In particular, it was
representatives of newer and more institutional interests who had caused resentment, and
the intention seems to have been to free people who held modest amounts of land from
what they saw as unjust and uncustomary impositions. In effect, it was a revolt against the
growth of government, but because the king at the time (Richard II) was a child, the rebels
could distance themselves from non-patriotic anti-royalism, and even argue that they
were the defenders of his real interests.

   Cambridge flourished in the twelfth and thirteenth centuries, and churches such as
Holy Trinity and St Botolph's were founded or rebuilt by the increasingly wealthy

41   St Botolph's, drawn by William Cole in the eighteenth century. Though it is very likely that an Anglo-Saxon church stood here, the earliest reused fragments are twelfth century and the roof has been dated by dendrochronology to 1200

burgesses clubbing together in gilds (**40** and **41**). It was money from this class rather than the aristocracy which supported the two religious houses, the leper hospital and the new St John's hospital. These years of growth were followed by a period of decline which lasted for much of the fourteenth and fifteenth centuries. Failure of corn crops in the early fourteenth century must have affected the markets, and the Black Death was a major contributor to the problems. Cambridge was notorious for its unhealthy climate and threats of pestilence until the late seventeenth century. At a national level there were wars with France and the civil wars of the Roses to disrupt trade and economic life. The coming of students did little for economic life, and in 1346 the town of Cambridge managed to avoid any contribution to the battle of Crècy, for example, by pleading poverty, like Oxford, because their population contained so many scholars and beggars. Changes to navigation and to economic patterns in England led to the growth of King's Lynn at the expense of the docks and hythes of Cambridge, and the only developments the town saw were those of religious houses and students hostels. These probably were of little direct benefit to the town, and the principal college development of these years, Henry VI's decision to build King's College, was for a long time a disaster.

By the end of the fifteenth century there were signs of prosperity returning, helped to some extent by the building works for the new colleges of Jesus and St John's. Cambridge was now preparing for the building boom, royal investments, and civic confidence that would mark the sixteenth century.

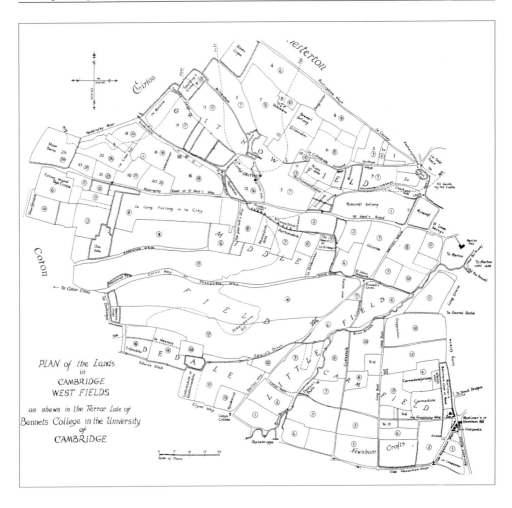

42   *The West Fields of Cambridge, drawn by Jack Ravensdale and Catherine Hall for Cambridge Antiquarian Record Society, based on a plan of 1789 and a thirteenth-century terrier*

Agriculture

Agriculture was organised on the basis of two great open arable fields which, with the land of the royal manor of Chesterton, encircled the settlement. These fields were known as the West, or Cambridge Field, and the East, or Barnwell Field. Arable land of the East Field came up to the occupied area, but the West Field was separated by meadows along the river. Within these fields the land was held as strips, each of which contained a variable number of selions, the unit of ploughing which we now recognise as ridge and furrow. Holdings were separated by grass-covered balks, used for access routes and fodder. There were generally no hedges or fences, although it was not unknown for crofts or closes to be taken out of the common fields either permanently or for a short time. This occurred particularly in the square and rectangular plots that seem to derive from older, possibly pre-Anglo-Saxon, field-systems around the hamlets of Newnham and Howes. Most of the selions were long and thin, covering about half an acre for ease of ploughing, but where there was an awkwardly-shaped area shapes known as gores and butts were devised to ensure that every piece of land was used. On the low-lying ground near to the town land was used for various grazing regimes, also organised on a common basis, so that all land-holders had rights to put certain numbers of animals onto them at certain times of the year. It is likely that most of the 373 households counted in the Domesday Book originally had rights in these open fields, though in later years this became unclear and overstocking was a constant problem. In the seventeenth century the town tried to restrict grazing rights to those with 'broad gates' but it is obvious that this was an attempt to rationalise an antiquated and half-forgotten situation.

Pressure for arable land was particularly great in the thirteenth century, and when a terrier of the West Fields was made for Corpus Christi in that century every scrap possible was being ploughed (**42**). As the population fell after the Black Death it was the lack of land suitable for grazing that was of most concern. Animals had to be sent to Fen edge villages such as Willingham to be fattened, and competition for the limited resources of the town was always ferocious. It led to some of the worst conflicts between the townsmen and institutional owners such as Barnwell Priory, and fear that meadow would be lost by private enclosures was the main issue in Ket's rebellion. Both Barnwell Priory and St Radegund's were probably founded on sites that had once been common land, which led to problems of access to routes which crossed them at times when the religious houses tried to assert private property rights. In 1275 and again in 1381, for example, the rights of all townsmen to drive cattle from Grenecroft (Midsummer Common) to Sturbridge across land held by Barnwell Priory was asserted.

The wild resources of Cambridge were also appreciated and carefully farmed. Holders of common rights, for example, had sole rights to grow willows along drainage channels, and there are many references to the profits made from this custom and to the measures taken to protect townsmen's privileges. Rights to fish in the Cam belonged to the town, which sold licenses to fishermen, some of whom can be seen at work on later maps, particularly that made by John Hamond. Within the built up area of the town, too, there were many places kept open for food production. Archaeological evidence shows that the rears of houses were generally gardens or yards, and documents confirm that owners of larger houses, the bishop of Ely for example, always included gardens and orchards in the properties. When the first maps of Cambridge were made towards the end of the sixteenth century, after several years of intensive building, many parts of the town were very rural, both in an ornamental way with gardens and fruit trees, and more functionally with farmyards, dovecotes, beehives, stable, barns and cattle sheds. There was a large group of fishponds in St John's College, and fishponds off Magdalene Street are known from the grant dating to 1428 to the abbot of Crowland. The religious houses were self-sufficient for much of their produce, and so were well equipped for agricultural and horticulture, as were manor houses, such as those of Harlestones, Mortimers and Merton.

At the end of the middle ages it was still farming and its associated pursuits that provided a living for most people and which dominated the environment. Arable open fields entirely surrounded the town, separating it from the surrounding villages. Between these and the settlement there were the marshy common pastures of Midsummer

Common and Jesus Green (both then known as 'Grenecroft'), Long Green (now mostly the Backs), Sheeps Green and Coe Fen, and the marshy area of the Coe Fen Leys and Swinecroft.

Trade

Most of the villages in southern Cambridgeshire were principally devoted to producing wheat and barley and, apart from what was used for food and drink, these crops had to be brought to market and exported, generally using waterways for ease of transport. Cambridge was the natural centre for much of this traffic. The abbeys of Ely and Ramsey used Cambridge as a collection point for grain for their vast landholdings in the county. Most of the exports were by water, but corn also went to London by road, via Ware. Imports to Cambridge, mostly coming into England from King's Lynn for re-distribution, were primarily sea-fish, wine and flax, and there were more local fenland products such as fresh-water fish and eels, turves of peat for fuel, rushes (universally used for strewing on floors), and sedge for heating ovens etc. Most of the hythes lay between Magdalene Bridge and the Mill Pool, but they extended as far down river as the present Rat and Parrot pub on Jesus Green, where waterfront structures dating from late Saxon and medieval times and from the eighteenth century have been excavated. Cambridge also served as a normal country market for its surrounding villages, and there were specific areas in the market-place reserved for stalls selling meat, milk, butter, cheese, poultry and vegetables. Several of these stalls gave their names to streets, for example, Butchery Row (now Guildhall Street), Slaughterhouse Lane (now Corn Exchange Street), and Cordwainer Street (Market Street).

The significance of Cambridge's trading position was recognised and promoted by an unusually early charter by Henry I in 1131, giving a monopoly on waterborne trade and the tolls paid at the hythes to the town. Later in the twelfth century the burgesses were able to pay the Crown a fixed sum to be free of various feudal taxes and restrictions, including meddling by the sheriff. This put them in a position to develop the commercial life of the town, and one sign of wealth at this time is the growth of annual fairs. There was a flourishing Jewish quarter near to Holy Sepulchre, which would have helped move the town into a higher league than serving local markets. Jews came to Cambridge soon after the Norman Conquest, and were lending money to merchants, and also to country landowners who wanted large houses in the town from at least 1140, and so were part of the building-boom. Their own homes were often built of stone, and there was also a synagogue on the site of the present Guildhall. Evidently their houses in this early period were spread through the town, for it is some distance from the area between Holy Sepulchre and the site of All Saints which was later known as the Jewry. Henry III appreciated the financial support the Jews had given him and issued proclamations for their protection, but his widow had some quarrel with them and in 1275 ordered their expulsion from any town where she had commercial rights. This included Cambridge, and so their wealth and expertise moved to Huntingdon.

Early in the thirteenth century the fair at Sturbridge was granted to the townsmen's leper hospital, and this alone provided wealth to their successors for centuries to come. Later in this century the wealth and independence of the town, so recently bought from

King John, began to be limited once again, this time in favour of the new university. Charters made at this time and in the fourteenth century for example, gave the university rights to supervise weights and measures and many aspects of the sale of food and drink, to set the levels of rent payable for town properties, and to take precedence over the mayor in many issues of jurisdiction.

It was in the fourteenth century too that Cambridge's importance for waterborne trade began to decline. Amongst the reasons for this were the larger draughts of the boats used for Continental trade, and also perhaps some silting-up of the river which, linked to a growing number of bridges, made shipping increasingly difficult. The sea-port of Lynn was developed as a more convenient point for the unloading and dispersal of cargo, with barges used for moving what was required to Cambridge. As Lynn was well-suited to the regular import and export of many more commodities than Cambridge, most notably wool from East Anglia, it grew considerably at this time at the expense of the markets in Cambridge. Only at Sturbridge did Cambridge maintain supremacy in long-distance trade.

Industry

Street names and occupations listed for townspeople give an impression of some of the manufactures in medieval Cambridge. Apart from the usual craftsmen and shopkeepers, we find mentions of people involved in stages of cloth production, and also scribes, illuminators and parchment makers. They undertook work such as rebinding and repairing the much-used manuscripts of the monks and scholars, and book-selling was always a profitable trade that university authorities were very keen to control. Pottery thought to be made in Cambridge in the late fourteenth and fifteenth century, though evidence for its site of manufacture is so far lacking, includes a distinctive and decorative ware known as sgraffito. These pots have a hard red fabric coated with buff slip, through which a pattern was incised before another glaze, yellowish with flecks of green, was applied (**43 and 44, colour plate 13**). There is some slight archaeological evidence for pottery kilns near to St Edward's church, and tanning pits have been found near St Benet Street. Both these anti-social land-uses would normally occur outside the town, so their occurrence suggests there was plenty of open space within the town, further evidence for the separation of clusters of early settlement. Even so, the neighbours must have been quite forbearing. These marginal areas that divided the parishes were also commonly used for quarrying gravel at this time.

Evidence for another unsavoury industry was discovered when the Arts Theatre, between St Benet Street and St Edward's Passage was excavated. This was a well containing the skinned and butchered remains of 79 young domestic cats, all dumped in the thirteenth century. We cannot tell whether this was a one-off event or a normal activity at the site, but we do know that cat fur was commonly used for hats, gloves and trims for other garments. Cats were not generally eaten, as these evidently had been, and so this may have been a time of famine, when they were considered acceptable, or they may have been deceptively sold as hare, which apparently they taste like and resemble once skinned.

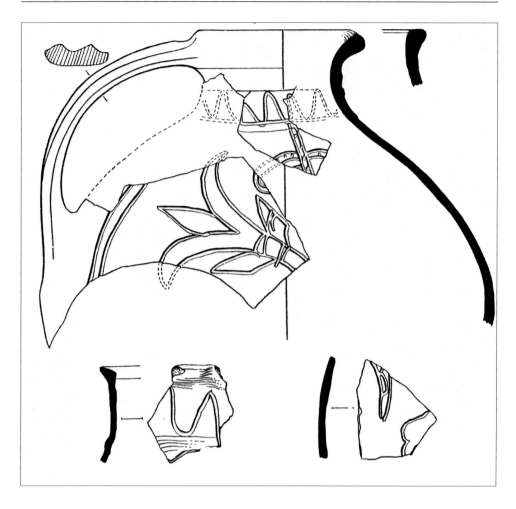

43   Cambridge sgraffito ware

Health, public services

Since the royal charter was given to Cambridge in 1268 the town was responsible for paving, drainage and general cleanliness, but there were always complaints about failures in this regard, lasting right up to the nineteenth century. In 1290 the chancellor did pave the town and levy a tax to pay for it. People were supposed to pave in front of their own properties, but the problems were immense. Accumulated dung left by all the cattle, pigs and horses that were brought into town overnight, for example, as well as the soiled rushes etc that had been used as floor coverings, were normally left in piles in the streets. Privies were built over the King's Ditch and, despite attempts to bring water into the town, it was more common to draw water from wells, and later on from pumps, often sited where the water ran through an overflowing churchyard, a state of affairs still common in the late nineteenth century. The unfortunate results of such insanitary habits were well known, but no attempts to stop them had any lasting effect. A royal writ in 1388 demanded that

44   A sgraffito sherd found on the site of Trinity College

the chancellor 'remove from the streets and lanes of the town all swine, and all dirt, dung, filth and trunks and branches of trees, and to cause the streets and lanes to be kept clear for the future', but it is clear from later comments, injunctions and charges against offenders that such demands had no more effect than modern attempts to lessen the similar nuisance of traffic on the streets.

The mid fourteenth century in Cambridge, as throughout England and much of Europe, saw the deadly and terrifying effects of the Black Death. Every level of society was at risk, and the town suffered more than the countryside, as it was to do in recurrent outbreaks over the next three hundred years, one of the significant factors that limited growth in this time. Half the scholars at King's Hall and most of the parishioners of All Saints by the Castle were among those who perished in the first outbreak, and there were many subsequent complaints of '*a sad mortality*'. It is thought that about half the inhabitants of the lower town died in the first outbreak, with a higher percentage in the upper town. The late fifteenth century brought new attacks, and scholars got into the habit of leaving for houses specially maintained in the countryside when sickness threatened. Henry VI refused to visit the town to lay the foundation stone for King's College chapel for the same reason. The poorly-drained open ditches of Cambridge, not least the King's Ditch, narrow dirty unpaved streets and a mobile population attending the university, markets and the fairs all helped make the town notorious for bad health. Proximity to the Fens with their mists and fevers, reaching to the marshes next to Downing Street, were also blamed, and a generally low standard of building before the sixteenth century must have left all levels of society vulnerable.

The town plan and its buildings

At the end of the Saxon period the framework of the medieval town was in place, but there were still gaps to be filled. The road-system consisted of a high street followed by numerous churches which converged with the old Roman through-route from the south-east, to which development was returning. Where these two roads joined there was a church known as St George's, in whose disused churchyard Holy Sepulchre (more commonly known as the Round Church) was built in the twelfth century. To the south, this road ran to Trumpington and then split into various routes to London, principally those going via Royston and Saffron Walden. One minor road that also joined it was Deepway, now Lensfield Road, running from the Trumpington Road to the south of the marshes known as Swinecroft. At their junction stood Dawes Cross. A similar medieval way-marking cross stood on the field road, Hinton Way, now Mill Road. Also converging on this road, near the Trumpington Gate and the church of St Botolph, was the road from south-west Cambridgeshire which crossed the river at the Small Bridges and which was itself joined by several east-westerly routes. By the early middle ages there was an important addition to this road-system; Milne Street, running parallel to the high street between it and the river, to which it was linked by numerous small lanes. Within the upper town on the opposite side of the river the Roman cross-road was still important to the road network. It was augmented with other long-distance routes, such as the road from the Isle of Ely that came via Histon and was known as the King's Highway. The road to Bury St Edmunds and Newmarket followed a ridge of higher ground, and along this the religious houses of St Radegund, Barnwell Priory and the leper hospital were built.

These routes were all forced to join the main Roman road before reaching the river so that they could cross at the Great Bridge, but that is not to say that the journey over it was always easy. Extra taxes were collected for a proposed stone bridge in the thirteenth century, but it was never built. The Hundred Rolls of 1279 record how planks were pulled from the half-rotten timber structure so carts fell in the river, enabling the keeper of the prison to make extra money running a ferry service. Orders to repair the bridge were constantly made in the fourteenth and fifteenth centuries. It was not until 1754 that a stone bridge was built, but this was still often in a poor state and led to many complaints. In 1823 a new iron bridge was made, which was rebuilt using the same design in 1983.

Excavations of the early town show that there was settlement outside the King's Ditch throughout the medieval period. Just beyond the Barnwell Gate, for example, at Bradwell's Court, there was a pit with Saxo-Norman St Neots and Thetford sherds and also two thirteenth-century wicker-lined pits. Near to Great St Andrew's there were four funnel-shaped pits with wicker-lined shafts reinforced with planks, probably wells, dating

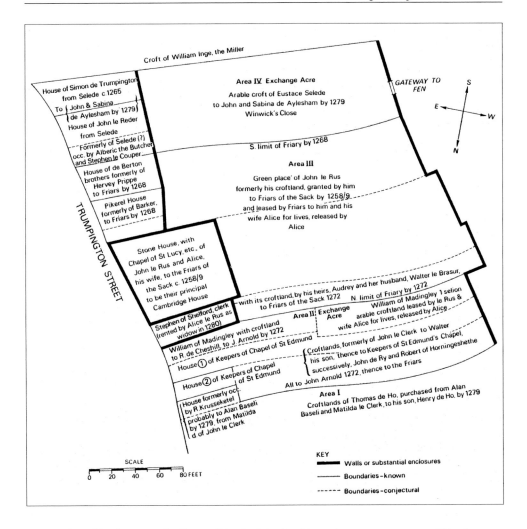

Croft of William Inge, the Miller

Area IV Exchange Acre

Arable croft of Eustace Selede
to John and Sabina de Aylesham by 1279

Winwick's Close

GATEWAY TO FEN

House of Simon de Trumpington from Selede c 1265

To { John & Sabina
{ de Aylesham by 1279

House of John le Reder from Selede

Formerly of Selede (?)
occ. by Alberic the Butcher
and Stephen le Couper

House of de Berton brothers formerly of Hervey Prippe to Friars by 1268

Pikerel House formerly of Barker, to Friars by 1268

S. limit of Friary by 1268

Area III

Green place' of John le Rus
formerly his croftland, granted by him
to Friars of the Sack by 1258/9
and leased by Friars to him and his
wife Alice for lives, released by
Alice

Stone House, with
Chapel of St Lucy, etc., of
John le Rus and Alice,
his wife, to the Friars of
the Sack c. 1258/9
to be their principal
Cambridge House

Stephen of Shelford, clerk
(rented by Alice le Rus as
widow in 1280)

William of Madingley with croftland
to R. de Cheshill, to J. Arnold by 1272

House ① of Keepers of Chapel of St Edmund

House ② of Keepers of Chapel of St Edmund

House formerly occ.
by R.Krusseketel
probably to Alan Baseli
by 1279, from Matilda
d of John le Clerk

with its croftland, by his heirs, Audrey and her husband, Walter le Brasur,
to Friars of the Sack 1272   N. limit of Friary by 1272

Area II Exchange
Acre

William of Madingley 1 selion
arable croftland leased by le Rus &
wife Alice for lives, released by Alice

Croftlands, formerly of John le Clerk to Walter
his son, Thence to Keepers of St Edmund's Chapel,
successively, John de Ry and Robert of Horningeshethe
thence to the Friars

All to John Arnold 1272, thence to the Friars

Area I
Croftlands of Thomas de Ho, purchased from Alan
Baseli and Matilda le Clerk, to his son, Henry de Ho, by 1279

TRUMPINGTON STREET

SCALE

0   20   40   60   80 FEET

KEY

▬▬▬ Walls or substantial enclosures

———— Boundaries – known

------ Boundaries – conjectural

45   *Plots of land given to the Friars of the Sack in the thirteenth century, now part of Peterhouse, reconstructed by Catherine Hall*

from the late eleventh to the fourteenth century. A reconstruction of the plots that were given to the Friars of the Sack on land outside Trumpington Gate shows how the curving strips of arable land there had already been settled by numerous homesteads (**45**).

During the twelfth century in particular the area between Milne Street and the river became the most populous part of Cambridge. It was packed with hythes and docks all along the river front, and with warehouses, granaries, houses, and a new church, St John Zachary, along the tiny lanes that ran through the area. The housing seems to have been a mixture of large houses with gardens, belonging to various gentry and to the prior of Ely, and small, tightly-packed properties much further down the social scale. One result of all this activity in an age when much of the refuse the occupants produced was tipped into nearby rubbish pits and so remained on the site, was that the ground levels rose by nearly

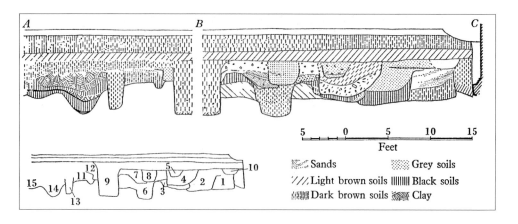

46 *A section recorded beneath Boots (next to Holy Trinity) is typical of the way land has risen throughout Cambridge where rubbish has been tipped for many generations*

two metres over the whole area. This phenomenon was later ascribed to deliberate acts by colleges when preparing low-lying land for development, but it is clear that it was the centuries of intense and rather filthy occupation that had an effect that has since been seen in many urban contexts. Occasionally this process might be undertaken deliberately for building foundations, but otherwise it was a useful by-product of tidying up the rubbish the town naturally produced. Pits to bury this waste are a major feature of excavations, particularly within low-lying college grounds, and tips of debris either in dumps or spreads are regularly found in archaeological and historical records. In 1475, for example, there was an agreement between the town and Queens' College allowing dumping of rubbish between the college grove and Newnham Road. From 1791-3 earth (and the bones it contained after many centuries of burial) was taken out of seven Cambridge churchyards and used on the Backs, to the western side of the river. This happened to be noted by John Bowtell, whose observations are preserved in manuscript form, but similar episodes must have been quite normal (**46**).

Growth continued into the thirteenth century, and the physical results of this are documented in a survey made in 1279. By this time there were 535 households and 76 shops, together with twelve agricultural barns or granaries, five university hostels and seventeen parish churches. The already-generous supply of churches had been augmented by St Peter by the Castle and St John Zachary. There was also a chapel in each of the religious houses, and the religious houses themselves were an important addition to the town, especially around its fringes. There was still a gap of relatively empty land around the marshy area south of the Great Bridge, and only a small number of parishioners were recorded there. A few years later, when further surveys were made for taxation purposes, the population here had more than doubled and this had also become the wealthiest area in the town. The substantial houses that the Jews had been forced to leave would have still been standing, and it was here that Roger de Harleston built a dwelling like a rural manor house, complete with dovecote and agricultural outbuildings. One thirteenth-century house was excavated in this area of Bridge Street and illustrates the high standards of some of the buildings here. Worked stone in its fabric included marble from Purbeck and from Hainault as well as Barnack stone, and there was stained glass in the windows. This must have been a particularly wealthy merchant's house and may well have belonged to one of the successful Jewish community.

The Jewish legacy of domestic buildings in stone was also the origin for the only significant public buildings other than churches to have a long and important history in Cambridge. The stone-built house of Benjamin the Jew was used as a gaol from 1224. The adjacent synagogue was given to the Franciscans who occupied it for about fifty years despite unhappy relations with their neighbours, until they acquired the site that was to become Sidney Sussex. The synagogue then became the Town Hall, generally known as the Tollbooth as collection of market tolls was a major function. It served until 1374, being then replaced with a simple meeting-room over open arches, where stalls were held. The gaol next door continued in use for misbehaving townspeople despite complaints about the primitive conditions there. University people fell under royal jurisdiction, and so would be imprisoned and tried at the castle. Also in this central area stood the stocks, and a pillory was put up when needed. The market cross was the site for official proclamations of all kinds.

Medieval domestic architecture has also left sadly little trace. Apart from the Green Man at Trumpington, a fifteenth-century timber hall hidden beneath sixteenth-century and later changes, the only exception to this generalisation is the stone hall known as the School of Pythagoras. This is a very interesting structure, dating to about 1200, built as a manor house and now subsumed in St John's College. It is a first floor hall, with an undercroft below, and was probably built by the Blancgernon family and purchased by Hervey Dunning, a wealthy Cambridge landowner who became mayor of Cambridge in 1207. In 1270 it was sold with about 180 acres to Walter de Merton in order to provide part of the revenues for his new college at Oxford. A dovecote, fish-ponds, ducks, geese, poultry, cattle and pigs were all recorded as part of the economy of this estate. There were extensive repairs, including rebuilding the west end in 1374-5, and a timber North Wing was added in the sixteenth or seventeenth century. After that, the stone house was used as a barn and became derelict, losing the vaulting of its undercroft in about 1800. It was a malting-house when a drawing was published in 1875. It was let for a time to Newnham college, and then as a private house before being converted into a theatre and subsequently a lecture hall by St John's, from 1960 onwards (**47**).

The late Middle Ages were difficult years for many towns that had no industrial base, though the wool towns of East Anglia grew large and rich at this time. In Cambridge, the whole town has signs of stagnation, but the problems were worst in the trading areas along the river. As the area became rundown it is likely that some of the wealthier inhabitants chose to leave what was now rather a squalid part of the town, and property values would not have been improved by crowds of impoverished students, happy to live several to a room, who would take over accommodation in any sort of condition. Like other dockland areas in this situation, land for redevelopment could be bought cheaply by a large institution with the vision and capital to make major changes. Then as now scholars might be poor but the colleges attracted powerful backers, and so, during the fourteenth,

47   The School of Pythagoras, drawn in 1875

fifteenth and sixteenth centuries, Milne Street and the whole of the town between the high street and the river became first student hostels and then some of Cambridge's most prestigious colleges. In this process, combined with the build up of soil discussed above, archaeological traces of the medieval town were covered over and can now only be seen when deep holes are dug (**colour plate 15**). Excavations within Trinity College, for example have uncovered waterlogged deposits containing worked wood, leather shoes and pottery sealed by the metalling for King's Childer Lane, which in turn became part of Trinity College in the sixteenth century, when the surface of the ground was deliberately raised with clunch blocks and rubble. Seventeenth-century drains and brick foundations for an ornamental garden were also discovered. In a similar way excavations on the front lawn of King's College in 1991 uncovered medieval lanes and tenements (mostly of timber but including an early fourteenth century brick building) and foundations of the Provost's Lodge in which Elizabeth I had stayed (**colour plate 16**). In this case the medieval buildings were shallow because they had stood until the nineteenth century and construction of the screen of King's College, but below them were more than 2m of built up layers above eleventh-century structures, a microcosm of archaeological riches in this sort of urban environment

7 The University

As Arthur Gray, Master of Jesus, described it in 1925 'Into this small town ... there tumbled a mob of 'clerks' ... they came suddenly and they brought no good character'. They arrived in 1209, having been thrown out of Oxford following murder allegations. There was no reason to welcome them to Cambridge, for they had little money, they could (and did) break the law without being subject to normal jurisdiction and, as young men who generally carried arms, they were involved in riots and disturbances of every kind. Quite why they chose to come to Cambridge is not known, and there probably was no single good reason. We know they tried Northampton and Stamford, and that Cambridge would have been home territory for some of them, for many Oxford graduates had been sent from Ely or were originally from Cambridge. Perhaps it was just that there was a shortage of moderate-sized towns with cheap lodgings available within range of this wandering gang where there was no central authority that could get rid of them or control their activities. In later years, the weakness of the town against both the university and the religious houses was certainly an important factor in their growth, and this was ensured by the steady backing of royal and other court powers.

Colleges of Piety
In looking at the development of the medieval university we have to bear in mind the inextricable confusion of religion and education it represents. The university itself functioned as an ecclesiastical body, with the chancellor being confirmed by the bishop of Ely and holding ecclesiastical powers, ie he had jurisdiction over all members of university and anyone in dispute with them, rights which were still maintained in the nineteenth century. The earliest founders were generally either church people themselves, or were seeking to further religious interests, for example by ensuring a supply of parish priests, clerks and educated monks who could preach and succeed in intellectual disputations. In the fifteenth century pious royals wanted both earthly glory and prayers for their immortal souls, motives similar to their ancestors who were the benefactors of churches from the tenth to the twelfth century, and religious foundations and hospitals from the twelfth to fourteenth. The future careers of most of those attending the university would likewise be linked to the Church, either as priests, monks in the religious houses who had sent them for an education, or as civil servants in holy orders. It was only after the middle ages that universities were used as finishing schools for rich gentlemen and providers of education for its own sake.

The lives of scholars also had much in common with those of monks in the later middle ages, for poverty and chastity might not be sought but they were usually inevitable, as students came from the middling classes of yeoman farmers and tradesmen and had to be supported for at least seven years. Many university men were also chantry or parish priests and others were monks or were training to become ones. Prayers and services were an important part of life in the colleges, just as study might be part of religious life. A communal life lived exclusively by adult men with unworldly aspirations in common was an ideal shared with monks, and so was the importance attached to living quarters of elaboration and beauty, however cold and uncomfortable they might be. The monastic design of rooms arranged around a cloister was considered the ideal, and the traditional importance attached to eating and drinking as a community, with high table reserved for the highest ranks and a long refectory-style table for all others, also has a monastic appearance, though the great style and opulence that became customary as soon as funds allowed must have surpassed even the comforts of late medieval Benedictines. This would have been the style of eating of lordly households before the changes to more private life-style in the later middle ages, and it is this custom which is probably the derivation of one of Cambridge's most enduring medieval legacies. It is even tempting to take the tradition further back, to the importance of the communal feast in Anglo-Saxon and Iron Age societies.

Another important strand that runs through the medieval university, reaching its peak in the sixteenth century but lessening thereafter, was the interest taken in it by the Crown and upper civil servants. Apart from reflected glory it was always necessary to have a supply of well-educated diplomats, administrators and clerks, so even kings with no other sympathy for learning knew they should support this institution — and if they forgot, then most of the members of their household were university men and would remind them. Officials such as the chancellors of the exchequer would almost certainly be graduates, and so were the royal confessors, which probably explains why queens and countesses were persuaded to give support.

In the early days the university consisted of small groups of boys and young men who attached themselves to a teacher and might then proceed to hire rooms or even a hostel where they could work and later live as cheaply as possible. Students would begin at the university in their early teens, working for at least seven years for a first degree, and then about ten more if they wished to progress to a Masters in theology or law, so something like a home-life was necessary for them. Also a community that could share books, resources and ideas provided essential support for scholars of all levels. Efficient church leaders were particularly concerned that their young monks had security and protection in hostels, though the early colleges were mostly intended for graduate students. It is therefore no coincidence that the colleges reflected monasteries in their architecture, and that the cloister/courtyard became the hallmark of the colleges they founded. The college courts, entered straight from the street by a simple but secure gate, consisted of the scholars' chambers on one side, always arranged vertically up a staircase rather than along corridors, a kitchen, buttery and dining hall opposite the gateway, a communal combination room, master's lodge and chapel, perhaps with a library fitted in at first floor level, on the third side, and more chambers, porter's lodge and the gate way adjoining the street. There were variants on this classic pattern but it proved an enduring model.

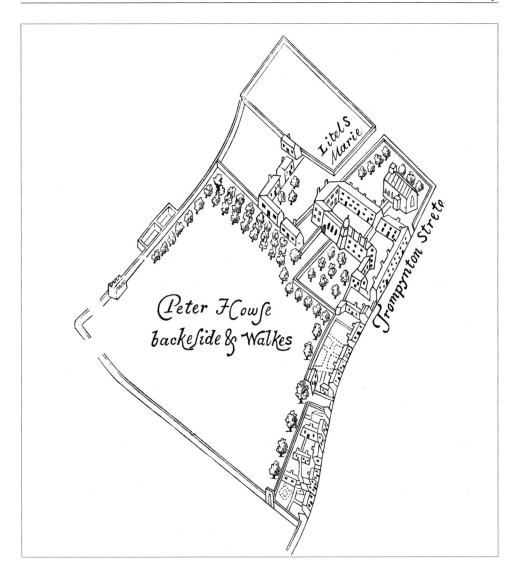

48   *Peterhouse in 1592. Little St Mary's was still being used as the college chapel and is shown linked by a walkway*

The first college, *Peterhouse,* was founded in 1284 by Hugh de Balsham, bishop of Ely. He had tried lodging his monks in St John's hospital, but no one was happy with this arrangement, and so Peterhouse Hall, now part of the south side of Old Court, was built (**48**). *King's Hall* was endowed by Edward II in 1317 in order to educate scholars known as the King's Childer as future civil servants, and in 1324 *Michaelhouse* (later subsumed in Trinity) was built by Hervey de Staunton, chancellor of the exchequer. *Clare* was founded soon after, in 1326, initially by the university chancellor and then later by the countess of Clare. Her statutes emphasise the training of priests 'in consequence of a great number of

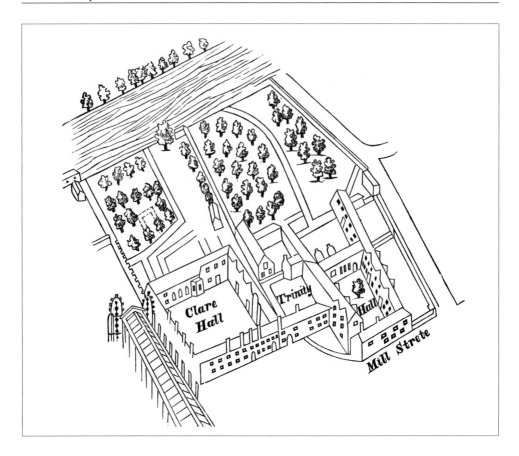

49   Clare College in 1592, when it just consisted of its original humble court

men having been taken away by the fangs of pestilence'. The original building works (**49**) have not survived. The Old Court was totally rebuilt from 1638-1715, its works being interrupted by the Civil War. Another countess, of Pembroke, endowed *Pembroke* College in 1347 (**50**). Its Old Court still has late fourteenth-century buildings, but ashlar facing was added in the eighteenth century, and the south and east ranges were demolished in the nineteenth century. *Gonville Hall* followed in 1348, built by a Norfolk clergyman, Edmund Gonville, in what is now the garden of Corpus Christi, being moved by his executor to the site of the present Gonville Court, itself much altered in later centuries. *Trinity Hall,* founded in 1350 by the bishop of Norwich, was intended to train clergy and lawyers for the Church and Crown, another response to losses due to the Black Death. Its Principal Court was built in the fourteenth century, though its ashlar facing and other changes in the eighteenth century hide this, except for original clunch visible in the north wall. The library is Elizabethan, but much of the college was rebuilt by Salvin and Waterhouse in the nineteenth century.

The Black Death, which caused the death of about half the parish priests when they were most needed for burial services and spiritual consolation, also inspired two gilds of

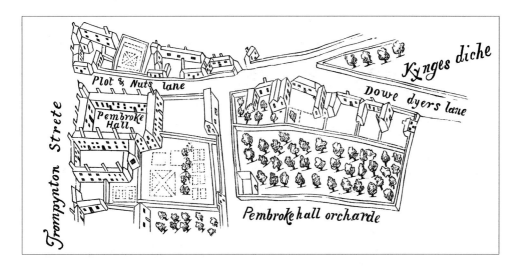

50   *Pembroke College in 1592, outside the King's Ditch, with generous areas for a formal garden and orchards*

Cambridge townspeople to pool their wealth to found *Corpus Christi* in 1352, specifically to ensure the training of more priests (**51**). Its Old Court of 1352–7 (**colour plate 18**), influenced by New College at Oxford, was the first complete Cambridge court, with a hall, kitchen, library, sets of private chambers and a master's lodge, but no chapel, as St Benet's served for this. In the next century Buckingham (later *Magdalene*) College was built in 1428 by the abbot of Crowland for his Benedictine monks who were studying here. Monks from Ramsey, Ely and Walden also attended (**52**). *God's House* was founded in 1439 by a London parish priest in order to train school teachers. It stood on part of the site of King's chapel and so had to be moved when building works began there.

A major departure in the tradition of college building came in 1441, when Henry VI began work on *King's* in order to provide further education for his scholars from Eton. Previous colleges had been built where hostels or other rights over property already existed or where parcels of land were cheap. In this process the commercial side of the town that adjoined the river was already changing its character, and the road running through it, Milne or Mill Street, had been interrupted. Henry took this process much further by acquiring a huge block of land and causing radical changes to the medieval town plan. Houses, shops and warehouses were cleared away, Milne Street was totally blocked, access to the river and its hythes was closed, and the church of St John Zachary, standing at the west end of King's chapel, was permanently removed. One of his acquisitions was the common meadow known as Long Green, on the opposite side of the river, the genesis of the Backs. He drew up plans of what he intended, and began work on the chapel. However the Wars of the Roses started in 1455, during which he was deposed and then murdered, and for more than three centuries most of his building site stood empty (**53**).

Queens' was in the more traditional style of foundation and construction. It was first founded in 1446 by the rector of St Botolph's, but subsequently became a royal

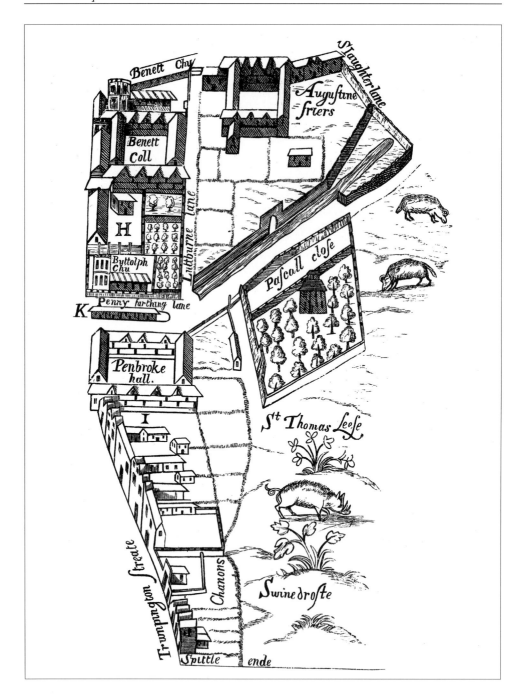

51   *Corpus Christi in 1574, here shown as Benett College after St Benet's church, which served as
its chapel. Note how the remains of medieval strip fields abut the marshes of St Thomas' Leys
and Swinecroft (where Downing College was later built), and the site of the Austin friars, vacated
forty years earlier, which is crossed by the King's Ditch. The house on the corner of Luttburne
(now Free School) Lane survived into the eighteenth century and is shown above (37)*

52   *The single court of Magdalene College in 1592, not long after Buckingham college was refounded as the only college on this side of the river. Sailing boats shown here were apparently still able to pass under the Great Bridge*

foundation, claimed for a short time by Margaret, wife of Henry VI and then by Elizabeth, wife of Edward IV. In the sixteenth century it expanded to take in the demolished buildings of the Carmelite friars. Its fifteenth-century Old Court is in the medieval monastic tradition, but just beyond is the irregular Cloister Court, belonging to several periods and best known for the President's Gallery of about 1540. As a contrast to Old Court this was built in the delightfully domestic half-timbered style this century favoured when it was not grand or martial, and as such is unique in Cambridge colleges (**54**). *St Catherine's*, founded in 1473 by a provost of King's, was intended to house priests who would pray for the provost's soul and study philosophy and theology, only becoming a teaching institution after the Reformation. It is therefore the last, and perhaps the most extreme case of a college founded humbly and for motives of piety. Unfortunately its buildings were so humble that they had to be totally rebuilt in the late seventeenth century.

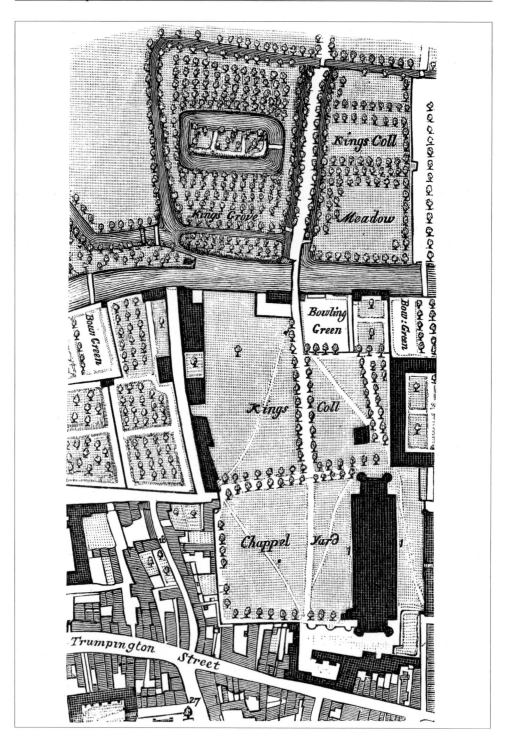

53   *King's College in 1688, when its spacious site had its chapel but no other buildings of note*

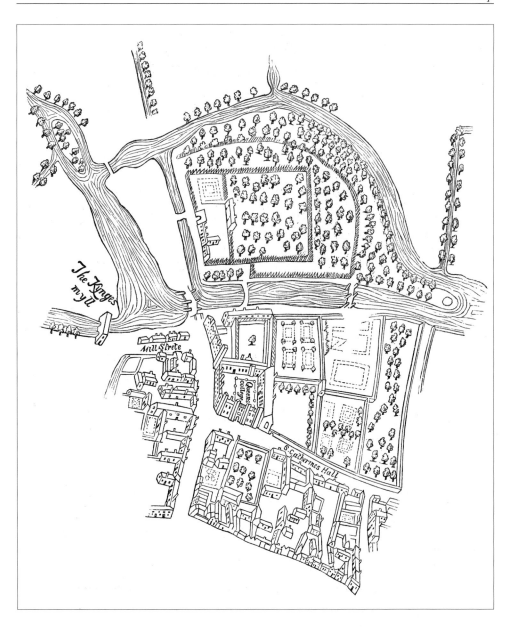

54   *St Catherine's and Queens' in 1592, with the King's Mill and a commercial area of the town*
      on one side and orchards and meadows on the other. The Carmelite site is just used as garden

55   The courtyard of the Old Schools in 1688

University buildings

Cambridge colleges have always been much richer than the university itself, and university buildings were therefore more simple. They consisted of a group known as the Old Schools, on King's Parade, and began as a single North Range on a site that was given in the late thirteenth century. They were put up between about 1350 and 1475 to house the schools of Divinity and Law, the library, and a Regent (or Senate) house with its chapel, and had been developed as a courtyard by about 1500. In the early eighteenth century James Gibb built the present Senate House next door, and the old east wing was then replaced with a new building. The library was extended in the nineteenth century. Many plans were made for this site, especially in the eighteenth century, but were abandoned on grounds of cost, and then eventually of taste. The university was able to build many more utilitarian structures in the nineteenth and twentieth centuries, but this is the area that has remained its heart and is the scene of degree-giving and other important ceremonies (**55**).

Colleges of Power

With the Tudor dynasty came a new attitude to the university, and more energetic involvement of royalty in the creation of colleges. Things started well, for the early sixteenth century was a time of religious reform and the university benefited from the realisation that improvements to education of clergy were important in combating the new Protestant heresies. Erasmus, already a scholar of international renown, came to study and teach from 1511–14, though he hated the town, university, and climate. John Fisher, holder of innumerable university posts including the chancellorship, was noted for his contributions to the new learning, especially the revival of Greek language and literature, before he was executed by Henry VIII. Buildings at this time reflected confidence, technical virtuosity, conservative good taste, and the need to make personal declarations of wealth and virtue. It is no coincidence that the world's finest surviving very late medieval building, King's College chapel, almost archaic in style when it was finished, dates to this period. The early sixteenth-century colleges were built as if they were semi-royal fortifications, with riotously decorative gatehouses commemorating their founders in real Tudor style. The gatehouses of Jesus, St John's, Christ's and Trinity are symptomatic of this age, decorated with personal crests, insignia and even names, combinations of the old symbols of military power in settings of monastic piety, with new yearnings for both individual aggrandisement and an association with the highest and most modern educational standards (**colour plate 17**).

Then Henry VIII divorced his first wife, changed the country from Catholicism to Protestantism, abolished the monasteries, and turned his dangerous gaze on the university. This was perhaps its most perilous time, for Henry, seeing them as semi-religious institutions, considered dissolving the colleges along with the monastic houses. Only adept string-pulling and some amazing accountancy, which convinced him that the colleges were too poor for him to bother with, saved them at this point and put them in a position to benefit from the misfortunes of their neighbours and previous friends.

Instead of abolishing them, Henry used some of the wealth of the monastic houses to bring a newly aristocratic style to the colleges, both in their architecture and functions. Universities began to attract young men from the higher classes who could afford a very different life-style to impoverished medieval scholars and, over the next four centuries, Cambridge came to be seen as a finishing school for the aristocracy and aspiring gentry. This change began gradually but many were concerned at adverse effects on academic life now that education was seen as an adjunct of royal patronage rather than of a religious life. Hugh Latimer, although a devout Protestant who would later be burnt for his faith, lamented 'it would pity a man's heart ... that we shall have nothing but a little English divinity, that will bring the realm into a very barbarousness and decay of learning, ... There will be none now but great men's sons in colleges ...', and in this last prophecy, for many centuries, he was not to be far wrong.

As direct royal involvement waned, colleges started to look more like good country houses, particularly as the sixteenth century wore on and the comforts of Elizabethan domesticity came to be appreciated more than her father's militarism. The last college in this series, Downing, was even set within a Capability Brown-type landscape and used the most fashionable architecture of its time, just like any other grand country mansion. An important element in the sixteenth-century phase of college building however, was the heritage they owed to the old monastic houses. In some cases this meant they were endowed with extraordinary wealth, for they took over the land and other investments of religious houses, and in others they had their valuable building plots. From the serious modern visitor's point of view, it is worth remembering that the rich sixteenth-century colleges along the Backs were able to afford the most extensive Victorian additions. It is

*56   Christ's College, in 1688, with the gatehouse on the street frontage and a dovecote in the rural
area beyond the court*

the older and poorer foundations on the outskirts that retain their medieval interest, and
those on old monastic sites that have the most tranquil grounds. In geographical terms,
the university grew to cover the whole of the riverside quarter, and by 1800 it virtually
encircled the remainder of the town.

Jesus College, founded in 1496 by John Alcock, bishop of Ely, might at first appear to hark
back to the pious foundations that were common earlier in that century, but the rapacious
style of its foundation by disinheritance of the nuns of St Radegund's and the grandiosity
of its construction, especially the gatehouse, are an early signal of more typically sixteenth-
century attitudes. The college was described by von Uffenbach in 1710 as lying 'quite out
of the town. It looks just like a monastery', and it was generally thought that the nuns'
medieval buildings had been taken over and reused. Recent investigations of the fabric
during restoration work, however, have shown that rebuilding was extensive and not
much of the fabric of the nunnery survives, the principal portions being the chapel and
other buildings that were made out of the nuns' church. The layout of Cloister Court,
though, and the spacious park-like landscape in its enviable situation immediately outside
the town, are features directly attributable to the nunnery.

Christ's College was founded in 1505 by Lady Margaret Beaufort, mother of the reigning
monarch, Henry VII. She took over what existed of the old God's House and built an
entirely new First Court. The original walls of this court were clunch and red brick but
they were later refaced in Ketton stone and so look much newer (**56**). As at Jesus, there is

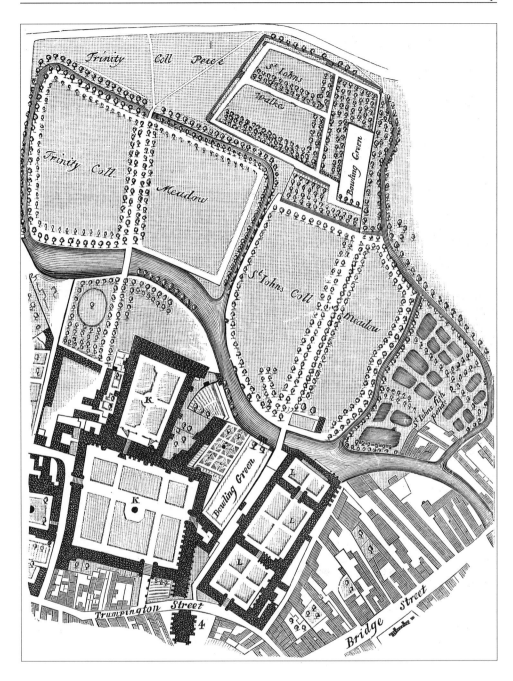

57   St John's and Trinity Colleges in 1688, including fish ponds, extensive areas of landscaped
      walks and lawns, and two bowling greens

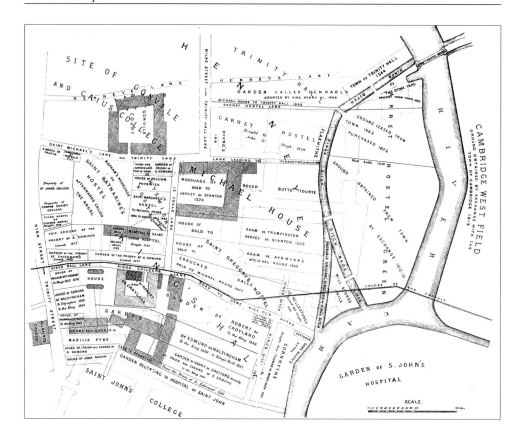

58   A reconstruction by Willis and Clark of the town before Henry VIII acquired land for Trinity College

a magnificent sixteenth-century gatehouse, in this case decorated with Lady Margaret's coat of arms, her statue, and the Rose of Lancaster. It stands on the street frontage, an imposing location for a statement of power by the new Tudor dynasty. Along with the gatehouse for St John's, her next foundation, these would have particularly impressed her grandson when he was persuaded to consider whether he might benefit from continuing Henry VI's work at King's.

St John's was founded like Jesus on the proceeds of a religious house, the argument this time being that the town's hospital was no longer serving a useful function, though the phrases used to justify closure are too suspiciously close to those used by Bishop Alcock for this to be taken literally. Like Christ's, the foundation is credited to Lady Margaret Beaufort, although it was John Fisher who was the moving force, and there was no need for extra endowment as the hospital had owned huge amounts of land that were taken over directly. These funds, with private donations, permitted extensive building works, and First and Second Court were completed in the sixteenth century (**57**). Unfortunately, the Victorians decided to improve upon the enclosure of First Court by pulling down its chapel, all that remained of the original church and infirmary, replacing it with a much less interesting building. They redeemed themselves, however, by building the most glorious trademarks of St John's, sometimes known as the 'Wedding Cake' buildings of New Court because of the exuberance and prettiness of their decoration.

It was Henry VIII's adoption of *King's* that set the pattern for the university as an aristocratic institution, though his success in actually constructing this college was limited to completion of the chapel that Henry VI began. He, too, left a beautiful building site where sheep continued to graze. Further plans were discussed for this college in the eighteenth century, but the Gibbs Building was the only result. It was not until the 1820s that William Wilkins was let loose to create the neo-Gothic splendour we have today. He went back to the grand sixteenth-century design of a monumental gatehouse, and set it within an ornate screen that from the street passes for one side of a traditional court (**colour plate 19**). A range was also built to the south which, with the screen, Gibbs Building and chapel, created Front Court. The Provost's Lodge and a row of half-timbered houses were taken down to accommodate this work.

Henry VIII, determined to surpass Cardinal Wolsey's foundation of Christ Church in Oxford, intended that his college at *Trinity* should be the most impressive in all of Oxford and Cambridge, and he endowed it with the wealth of twenty-four monastic houses. King's Childer Lane, Flaxhythe Lane, and Foul Lane were built over, and Flaxhythe itself, once a branch of the river, was infilled. Michaelhouse and King's Hall (itself incorporating the school of the King's Childer and including King Edward's tower) became part of the new foundation (**58**). Like King's, Trinity College was left unfinished (**59**), for Henry died soon after its foundation, and the college was principally the result of work by its masters, Nevile in the sixteenth, Bentley in the eighteenth and Whewell in the nineteenth centuries. The chapel is Elizabethan, in very late Gothic style, using stone from the Franciscan friary and from Ramsey abbey. The oldest part of the college is King Edward's tower, 1428-32, which was moved twenty metres north by Nevile, master from 1593-1615 (**colour plate 20**). He was the builder of Great Court and Nevile Court, the latter being three-sided until Wren built a library on what had been an island, Garret Hostel Green. The north and south ranges were then extended to meet the new library. In the eighteenth century Essex rebuilt the north and south ranges in classical style to match Wren's work. Wilkins built New Court in neo-gothic fashion, and neo-Tudor Whewell's Court was also added in the nineteenth century.

Under Elizabeth most of Cambridge seems to have been fairly broad-minded with regard to religion, with only hard-core Catholics eventually losing college posts as the century wore on and positions became more polarised. Cambridge contained well-known Catholic sympathisers as well as the Puritan colleges of Emmanuel and Sidney Sussex. John Keys(who Latinised his name to Caius) is a good example of how a Cambridge man could survive religious controversy. After studying at Gonville he travelled widely in Europe, and then made his money as royal physician before being dismissed by Elizabeth for maintaining Catholicism. This did not prevent him returning to Cambridge where he refounded his college as *Gonville and Caius* and became its master, undertaking extensive building works. He introduced the idea of the three-sided court, partly for hygienic reasons, and also the three gates of Humility (now moved to Master's Garden) Virtue and Honour, which are redolent of renaissance symbolism in a truly Elizabethan way.

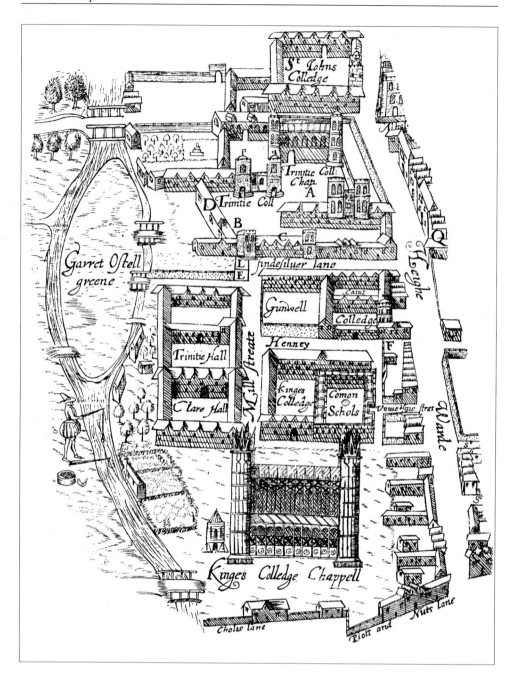

59   *Trinity College in 1574, with the chapel complete but none of Nevile's works begun. Note the island of Garret Hostel Green, where the library was later sited, the bell tower west of King's chapel and the buildings to the east (whose foundations sometimes appear as parchmarks), and the man fishing by the river*

60   Pepys library at Magdalene, engraved by W Westall in 1815

Buckingham college was abolished when the monasteries were dissolved, but the site was given to the lord chancellor, who was also made Lord Audley of Walden, and he was given permission from Henry VIII to refound it as *Magdalene* College in 1542. Its First Court mostly dates to the fifteenth-century monastic phase, apart from the Pepys library, which forms one side of the courtyard (**60**). Work started on this library in the late sixteenth century, using the style of an Elizabethan house, and finished in the early eighteenth century in order to house the books that Samuel Pepys bequeathed to the college, and which can still be seen in their purpose-made book-cases. When Magdalene wanted to expand in the 1950s the only space it could use was on the opposite side of Magdalene Street, where there was a huddle of picturesque old houses and factories. As it was never a rich college, some of these buildings were converted rather than demolished, including a vinegar factory and some sixteenth-century cottages that are now sets of rooms for undergraduates. Pretty cottages on Fisher Lane, however, one of the last of Cambridge's hythes, were lost in this development.

Emmanuel was the first college to be founded after the Reformation was complete in England, and was in the new Puritan tradition. Elizabeth I resisted any temptation to create colleges herself despite the religious sites standing empty at the time, but her chancellor of the exchequer was perhaps feeling the lack of qualified clerks, and in 1584 he took over the old friary of the Dominicans, standing outside the town and now deserted for more than forty years. Only parts of the church and refectory seem to have

61   Sheep being driven past Emmanuel College, from an engraving by le Keux in 1841

been reused, and these were heavily disguised so there was no hint of its Catholic antecedents (**61**). *Sidney Sussex* was another Puritan foundation, this time using the ruinous site of the Franciscans house. It was built with a bequest from the Dowager Countess of Sussex in 1594, and was originally designed like a large version of an Elizabethan country house. Heavy restorations, additions, altered layout and other changes in the nineteenth century, including covering the whole building in cement, have hidden this. Like Emmanuel, it enjoys a spacious location outside the academic quarter by the river (**62**).

In the second half of the seventeenth century, with the restoration of the monarchy and many other of the old institutions, aesthetics were once again seen to be important and appropriate decoration was no longer a sin. In this climate Matthew Wren employed his young nephew Christopher to design his first building, Pembroke chapel, and the new classical style became popular for much restoration work and additions to college buildings in the eighteenth century (**colour plate 21**). Aesthetics may have been important, but academic life was in a poor, even scandalous state in the eighteenth century in particular. Various reports of this time, borne out by official figures, give a grim picture of declining standards, which is perhaps most graphically described by a German visitor. In 1710, von Uffenbach described the university as a whole as 'certainly very bad. We were amazed that no courses of lectures at all are delivered, and only in winter 3 or 4 lectures are given by the professors to the bare walls, for no one comes in, ... in summer scarcely anything is done, both students and professors being either in the country or in London.' The

62   Sidney Sussex designed like a large country house, engraved by le Keux in 1841

impression he gives is that the only teaching was by private tutors, and the only students were noblemen or otherwise wealthy men. This was not entirely true, but standards were definitely low for the majority who chose not to work. As Isaac Newton showed in the late seventeenth century, however, facilities were there for exceptional men to progress to great heights, and the introduction of professorships in, for example, chemistry, astronomy, anatomy, modern history, botany, geology and medicine widened the opportunities for learning immensely. Von Uffenbach was also scathing about individual colleges, and in particular their libraries, in which he had come to work and which generally seem to have been in a very neglected state. He even complained about dining in hall at Trinity, which he described as 'very large, but ugly, smoky, and smelling so strong of bread and meat, that it would be impossible for me to eat a morsel in it. On both sides there are placed long, narrow tables, and wooden benches', though the library 'could not be handsomer or more convenient'. He was even less impressed with Magdalene. 'It is one of the meanest here, of which the King James used to say in jest, that he would go to stool there. It is a very old, and, as I said, mean building; the library ... is also very small, and may perhaps contain 600 volumes. All ... entirely overgrown with mould'. Corpus Christi was also 'an old and poor building, indeed one of the ugliest colleges, lying entirely among the houses, so that one cannot see it', though he admits that it contained the 'choicest manuscripts'. Declining student numbers were another feature of these years, even though their quarters were being made so much smarter and more spacious. Numbers of graduations, which had

63   *Downing College, engraved by W Westall in 1815, soon after it was built. It is a late example of the classical style, designed to have the landscaped setting of a large country house*

been about five hundred a year in 1600, were down to about one hundred in 1800, though they regained then surpassed the former numbers in the mid nineteenth century.

Much work was also undertaken in this century to repair, update and augment the colleges and university with new or improved buildings, but there was a long gap before Downing College was finally founded in 1800. A fortune had been left by Sir George Downing, but there were long years of litigation with his family before the college was finally built. The architect was Wilkins who used the classical style that was still fashionable to build on the spacious rural site (**63**). Only a small proportion of what he intended was built, and later additions changed his concept of individual buildings set within landscaped lawns into more normal ranges. The site was originally designed to have a grand entrance from Downing Street, but financial constraints forced the college to sell land closest to the town to the university in the late nineteenth century, so the plan had to be turned round, resulting in a modest side-gateway from Regent Street.

With the new century there was boredom with severe classicism in the arts and an increasing taste for medievalism, and with revolution in Europe linked to violent anti-clericalism, Catholicism suddenly stopped being seen as a subversive foreign threat and instead was thought of almost as an ally of conservative (and especially aristocratic) forces in Britain. A combination of these moods meant that not only were medieval styles now fashionable and romantic, but they were also seen as more authentic, historical and altogether more virtuous. The combined appeal to romantic susceptibilities, antiquarian interests and defence of privileges had a huge effect in both Cambridge and Oxford. It

64   *The popular view of Girton College, built for women when at last they were allowed within three miles of Cambridge*

affected poets such as Wordsworth, who studied here. It generated increasingly High Church reforms to the moribund Church of England and its collapsing churches, and above all in Cambridge its impact on architecture is all around us. Nowadays, it is mostly the Victorian Gothick of St John's from the Backs, the reconstructed Holy Sepulchre usually known as the Round Church, and Wilkin's screen and gatehouse at King's that are most photographed as archetypal Cambridge.

Towards the middle of the nineteenth century there were strong demands for change within the university itself, particularly to its academic and teaching standards. Much of the pressure came from outside, especially from the government and royalty in the form of Prince Albert. Reforms were slow, but huge changes did occur throughout the century, and student numbers grew again. More subjects were introduced, especially in the new scientific fields, teaching staff increased, even sons of noblemen had to sit some sort of exam before being awarded a degree (though any sort of entry criteria were successfully opposed), entry was opened first to Nonconformists and then Catholics and Jews, and there were even some concessions to women although it would be half a century before degrees were first awarded to them in 1948. A far-reaching reform in 1882 meant that at last fellows could marry. There were many building programmes, for example converting the old Botanical Gardens on the site of the Austin priory into the New Museums Site, and creating the great Cambridge museums, such as the Fitzwilliam, Archaeology and Anthropology, and the Sidgwick Museum of Earth Sciences. Most colleges were altered or enlarged at this time, and new ones were founded, including the women's colleges of Girton and Newnham (**64**).

8 The Cambridge Fairs

In addition to the regular market and constant trading activities of the Cambridge merchants there were four annual fairs, all of them held outside the medieval town. One of these, Sturbridge Fair, gained international renown as Britain's greatest commercial gathering, and two others, Reach Fair and Midsummer Fair, are still flourishing as annual events more than 800 years after they began.

Reach Fair, held in a hamlet on the Fen edge about ten miles from Cambridge but with easy transport along waterways, was given a royal charter in 1201, though it is much older than this. It lasted for three days at Rogationtide, which succeeded the pagan festivals of May Day. The site had been a Roman port, and became a settlement that had no church and was not a parish, though its location at the end of Devils Dyke, the great Anglo-Saxon defensive earthwork, must have given it the commercial opportunities often found in settlements in frontier zones. It may have been growing into a market before the Norman Conquest, and was certainly flourishing well before its acquisition by the Cambridge authorities.

Reach was one of Cambridgeshire's inland ports from the middle ages until the nineteenth century, with trade in timber and iron from Baltic countries in particular. Corn was always an important export, and clunch, a kind of hard chalk used in various Cambridge buildings, was quarried here and in nearby villages. Hythes and basins were made to accommodate this trade, and a Fair Green was made by levelling part of Devils Dyke. In 1511, when the first financial statement is recorded, the profits were only 6s 2d, and it was obviously really just an excuse for an outing of the corporation. Later on, this was disgracefully the case, for feasting and parades were on a particularly extravagant scale while trade steadily declined in the eighteenth century, though imports of coal, wine, timber and bricks continued to be recorded. Amusements became a more important part of the proceedings, and the fair continued to be opened by the mayor and corporation with pomp and feasting. Even now the fair is still opened by the mayor every May, and there is still horse-trading in addition to a fun fair, though Reach itself is once again a quiet rural settlement.

Garlic Fair, held in mid August, (the Christian festival of the Assumption, or pagan Lammas) stayed a low key event, but it too was long-lived and must have had more economic and social significance than we can find in the records. It was granted to the nuns of St Radegund's in the mid twelfth century, and was held within the extensive grounds of the nunnery, first on a site next to Jesus Lane where it was entered by a gate through a 'mud wall'. The master's garden was later extended over this area, and the fair moved to the junction of Park Street.

65   *'Pot Fair', drawn by H W Bunbury in 1777*

Midsummer Fair was granted to Barnwell Priory in 1211, to be held from 22-25 June, but like Reach its antecedents are undoubtedly much earlier than this, as its date during the pagan midsummer festivals suggests. The Priory itself was sited by a sacred well at a place where it was already noted by the Barnwell chroniclers that 'boys and lads met to amuse themselves in the English fashion by wrestling matches and other games and applauding each other in singing and playing musical instruments', gatherings where traders would naturally also be present. These rituals were brought under control with a combination of Christianity and more organised commercialism but the elements of fun and limited lawlessness were still permissible. The burgesses of the town started to take over this fair in the middle ages, and had complete control after 1506. Alderman Newton, who kept a diary in the seventeenth century, recorded its traditional opening, at which he was present in 1669. After plenty of cake, wine and beer 'Mr Mayor and the Sergeant and Bayliffs in their Gownes and the Aldermen and the 24ty in their Cloakes went from Mr Mayors to the fayre to the Booth there', and after another change of gowns proceeded to 'proclaime the fayre in 2 places' before changing clothes and dining again.

Attractions at this fair in 1714 included Punch, a giant, a dwarf, wild beasts, dancing dogs, three-legged cats and a female rope-dancer. By the late eighteenth century it was particularly known for selling pottery, after which it acquired the name of Pot Fair (**65**). At about this time it was extended from four days to a fortnight each year, and became more profitable to the town than Sturbridge. It was a very fashionable resort at this time for both town and university, partly because it then occurred when undergraduates' relations were in town. Henry Gunning, writing his reminiscences of the late eighteenth century, recalls how 'The fair on Midsummer Green, known by the name of 'Pot Fair', was in all its glory. There were booths at which raffles for pictures, china and millinery took place every evening, which were not over until a late hour. The Saturday evening preceding the Commencement brought together the greatest assemblage of company; the gentry in the town and neighbourhood, and many persons from adjoining counties used to be present ... groups of Masters of Art consisting of four or five in a party, *who had evidently dined*, were to be seen linked arm-in-arm and compelled all they met with to turn out of their way'. Primitive roundabouts, propelled by hand and then by horses, were seen at this fair in the eighteenth century.

By the mid nineteenth century Midsummer Fair, like all the fairs, was in decline and became only four days again, though it was to remain a popular part of the town's summer calendar. Increasingly, amusements took over from the traders, a return to the earlier functions in a sense, though horse trading was still important at the end of the nineteenth century. Rides became more exciting when steam-power worked them after 1870, and freak shows, boxing, wrestling and moving picture shows are all mentioned as part of the proceedings. A newspaper description in 1901 commented on the level of 'the stir, the noise and the mirthfulness', and these are things that have not changed. Nowadays it mostly attracts its huge crowds for its rides, nearly fifty in number, many of them of the white-knuckle kind, and there are still plenty of stalls with wares for sale, even with crockery of cheap and cheerful kinds as before, and side-shows include fortune-telling, shooting, coconut shies etc. Its main audience is the young, out to enjoy itself amid an amazing level of noise, in many ways a return to its ancient past. Still, too, the mayor and corporation scatter pennies to the crowd at midsummer and open the proceedings in style, though their feasts are not up to eighteenth-century standards.

It was Sturbridge Fair, however, its origins unknown apart from a charter for the town's leper hospital to hold a market granted by King John in 1211, that put Cambridge on the national and international stage for more than 500 years. Some of the economic advantages of its location and legal situation are obvious, but the reasons behind its phenomenal growth are hard to understand. One important factor was the site's position adjacent to the river, where barges from King's Lynn and the Wash could unload directly, and it was also on an important east-west route heading for Newmarket, serviced by a regular ferry across to Chesterton. The site was therefore accessible from most of England, was reasonably central to the nation, and its position close to a lively town was also an asset. Its only overriding advantage, however, seems to have been largely negative; there was simply no individual or authority which could impose many limitations or taxes on it and so it was, in general, free to grow.

It belonged to the town burgesses after the hospital ceased to function in the late thirteenth century, and these individually owned the right to hold booths or stalls. These stalls became very profitable assets, which gave the townsmen collectively an incentive to encourage expansion of the market and to resist calls by university authorities for more controls on behaviour. A court, known as the Pie Powder (or *pied poudre,* 'dusty feet'), held on the site by the burgesses, sorted out the minor nuisances that can spoil mass activities,

66   Typical booths at Sturbridge Fair, drawn in 1832

but the town council was far too inefficient a body to seriously limit commercial or social initiatives, and the university mostly just came here to enjoy the fun. Sturbridge, too, had the good fortune to be held at the right time of year, immediately after harvest, timing which in fact was forced by its situation on the arable open fields. The agreement, described by Daniel Defoe in the eighteenth century, was that if the crops were not cleared by the right day, the stall-keepers could enter and trample them. Similarly if the fair was not cleared away in time then the ploughmen could come in with cart and plough and destroy the stalls. This date after harvest meant that there were plenty of crops to be sold, people had leisure and money, and travel was comparatively pleasant and convenient. It was also outside term-time, so tradesmen and others whose customers or employers were absent had time to spare.

The fair was originally held for two days in mid September, expanding to last from 24 August to 29 September by 1516, an illustration of its success in the middle ages. There are no eye-witness descriptions of the fair in these years, and our knowledge of it is mostly drawn from the financial accounts of those who bought goods there. Its social aspects can be deduced from the comments of later visitors, and we can imagine how these might be welcomed as the life within the limits of the town came increasingly under the influence of religious houses and the university.

Timber and iron, presumably Baltic exports, were bought for Cambridge castle in the late thirteenth century, and fourteenth-century accounts list fish, horse-shoes, mats, baskets and cloth. Early in the fifteenth century the organisation of the various booths was an issue in the official record books, and the impermanent layout of the fair was nevertheless fixed enough for street-names to be used. Foreign goods and products from London were now being sold, and luxuries such as silk and gold-embroidery were bought alongside timber, iron and fish from the Fens and from the North Sea fleets. London merchants were both buying and selling, estates in the country stocked up for the year here, and the nuns at St Radegund's recorded buying pepper, soap and a churn as well as staples such as timber and fish. From town accounts of rents from the fair it is clear that organisation of the booths was fixed as if it was a town, not structures rented in a ploughed field (**colour plate 22**). 'The Duddrye', 'Birchin Lane', 'Chepesyde', 'Hadley Rowe', 'Back Boothes', and 'Bury Boothes' are listed for 1561. The booths themselves had to be set up in the approved fashion and order every year, by carpenters who had a fortnight to get everything done and who would never take on other work at this time, as college masters had to learn. They were made of timber frames and deal (pine) boards, with hair-cloth used for roofs and fronts, fitted with counters and shelves, with a protective awning in front and a small room with beds for the stall-keepers behind (**66**).

In this century the town had to contest its rights over the fair with both the Crown and the university, and a new charter in 1589 agreed the university's right to control the quality of merchandise while the town had all the profits and legal rights, apart from cases involving members of the university. The description of the fair in this charter stated that it 'far surpassed the greatest of and most celebrated fairs of all England; whence great benefits had resulted to the merchants of the whole kingdom, who resorted thereto, and there quickly sold their wares and merchandises to purchasers coming from all parts of the Realm'. Apart from the money made by individual burgesses from the booths which they owned, the town was supposed to use all profits to pay its tax to the Crown and to cover costs of 'its ways, streets, ditches and other burthens'. However, descriptions from later years suggest that a large proportion must have been used for the food and drink the corporation consumed during the event, even before other forms of corruption intervened.

Sturbridge Fair entered English literature as the model for John Bunyan's *Vanity Fair*, and there are references to it by Samuel Pepys and other seventeenth-century commentators, but the first surviving eye-witness account was published as a pamphlet, *A Step to Stir-Bitch-Fair*, by Edward Ward, in 1700. He describes how he walked to 'a renown'd Village which by all reports very deservedly gain'd the Ignominious Epithet of Bawdy-Barnwel, so call'd from the Numerous Brothel Houses it contains for the Health, Ease, and Pleasure of the Learned Vicinity ... where I beheld such as number of Wooden Edifices, and such Multitude of Gentry, Scholars, Tradesmen, Whores, Hawkers, Pedlars and Pick-Pockets, that it seemed to me like an Abstract of all sorts of Mankind'. In his wanderings through the fair his 'Nostrils were saluted by a Saline, Savoury Whiff ... I came into a Dutch Market of red and pickled Herrings, Salt-fish, Oysters, Pitch, Tar, Soap etc ...' and he came across 'slit-deal tenements occupied by Sempstresses, Perfumers, Milleners, Toy-men, and Cabinet-makers; ... Powder'd Beau's, Bushy Wig'd Blockheads, Country Belfa's, and beautiful Bury Ladies...' Books were sold (or stolen in the scholars' long-sleeved gowns), whole libraries auctioned, and in the street called Cheapside there were many 'wholesale Tradesmen, as Linnen Drapers, Silk-men, Iron-mongers, Leather-sellers, Tobacconists etc', not to mention the London citizens, supposedly here to meet customers but with little to do but 'Drink, Smoke and Whore'. In the square known as the Duddery, cloth was sold wholesale, and wool was in huge bags estimated with some exaggeration as 'Tun Weights'.

Daniel Defoe, in his *Tour through the whole island of Great Britain*, first published in 1724, gives a very useful and clear account of his visit to the fair, which he describes as the greatest in the world, though admitting that he cannot compare it with the German fairs which he has not seen. He describes how the shops were arranged in rows, like streets, 'goldsmiths, toyshops, braziers, turners, milliners, haberdashers, hatters, mercers, drapers, pewterers, china-warehouse, and in a word all the trades that can be named in London; with coffee-houses, taverns, brandy-shops, and eating-houses innumerable'. His description of the wool-market held in the square called the Duddery is particularly important for, whilst writing of 'vast warehouses piled up with goods to the top', and the sale of £100,000 worth of goods in less than a week, he also mentions that wholesalers from all over England were taking orders and receiving money 'wholly in their pocket-books', and these paper sales were now far more than the actual goods brought to the fair. This method of dealing would inevitably change the commercial value of all such fairs, and would lead to their decline. There was little evidence for any such problems at this stage however and, apart from wool, another commodity for which Sturbridge was the national market and price-setter each year was hops, mostly brought in from Surrey and Kent for sale to northern England. Other goods arriving by barge included 'wrought iron and brass ware from Birmingham; edged tools, knives etc from Sheffield; glass ware, and stockings from Nottingham, and Leicester'.

Towards the end of the fair, the social side took over and 'the gentry came in, from all parts of the county around'. Entertainments mentioned are 'puppet-shows, drolls, rope-dancers, and such like'. The last day was the horse fair, with horse and foot races for the 'meaner sort of people only'. Less than a week later, piles of dung and straw, valuable to the ploughmen, were all that was left of the fair.

When Henry Gunning, then in his eighties, wrote his reminiscences in 1849, he had to wrack his brain to remember Sturbridge Fair when he used to visit as a town official in the late eighteenth century, for it had changed so much since then. He notes in particular the road that was lined with cheese stalls, dealing in the produce of Cottenham, Willingham and other Cambridgeshire villages, as well as the other cheese producing counties, with many of the sales being sent on to London. He too describes the wool-market of the Duddery, but says that it was beginning to decline then. Hop sales still took up a lot of space, and so did earthenware and china from the Potteries and from Ely. A row stretching from Newmarket Road to the Chesterton Ferry included 'silk-mercers, linen drapers, furriers, stationers, an immense variety of toys, and also of musical instruments'. It is easy to see how a city could have taken root here if conditions of land-tenure had been different, or if Enclosure and the sale of parcels of land happened a few years earlier. There was also 'the usual mixture of dwarfs and giants, conjurors and learned pigs', (very learned in fact, as Gunning admits that he and other members of the university set their owners up with questions and answers to embarrass some of the audience). Food and drink were a very important part of the entertainment, and at last, after 1740, and after persistent opposition from the university, a theatre was allowed here, with 'many respectable, and frequently excellent performers'.

By the mid eighteenth century, however, the fair had passed its peak. From then on, tax returns suggest a smaller income for the town though its social side hardly seems to be affected. In 1772 Caraccioli, in *An Historical Account of Sturbridge etc*, notices how changing patterns of trading have affected the fair, which now lasted only a fortnight. Some streets, for example the booksellers, had gone, presumably because they were now working through shops. More sophisticated marketing and banking systems generally were making large annual fairs outmoded for wholesale dealing in commodities, and shops in towns were also increasingly able to supply customers needs more conveniently. During the eighteenth century too, access to a navigable river ceased to be such an unusual and valuable asset. Turnpike roads changed patterns of mobility, and canals opened up areas situated closer to the newly industrialised sites in the midlands and northern England, whilst Cambridgeshire itself could still boast no more than agricultural produce. Even cloth production was shifting from East Anglia to the North in this period.

Then Cambridge fell into the hands of the Mortlock family, and the lasr booths became private property, so that the town had no direct benefit from the fair. In the 1790s the civic procession was abandoned and organisation was neglected. Its festive aspects, including the theatre until it was declared unsafe and demolished in 1803, and the relaxed atmosphere away from some of the university's restrictions, were still appreciated, but its commercial strengths had gone as the nineteenth century began.

The medieval open fields on which Sturbridge Fair was held were enclosed in 1811 and, although all the rights relating to the fair were retained, the plots of land were now held by individuals who were free to sell to developers or to use them as they wished. At this time, land close to Cambridge that was freed up in this way and was not controlled by the university was valuable, and parts of it were soon built upon or their clay soil was quarried for bricks. When the railway came, built on the site of the old Duddery and other booths, it made the fair even more obsolete as a commercial centre. The fair could still draw the public to spend money on enjoying themselves after harvest-time, but retail shops were increasingly being set up in central Cambridge, and these expected to benefit from the extra custom it brought to the town, rather than seeing it as competition. Josiah Chater, who founded a successful business with his brother in the mid nineteenth century, kept a diary at this time, and he records how they set up stalls in the yard adjoining their shop to cope with this extra trade. '25th September, 1848. Sturbridge Horse Fair Day. Business has been exceedingly good, and the leather and horse fair being condensed has made us doubly busy'.

At this time, too, the fair was decreasing to only a few days in length. In this, and in its concentration on pleasure rather than commercial activities, Sturbridge paralleled most of Britain's once-great fairs at this time, though it is unusual in fading away so completely before its abolition in 1933. One reason was probably its location in 'Bawdy Barnwell', which became a rougher area still with the surge in population after Enclosure. It was no longer an area where newly respectable Victorians might choose to go, and the pennies that labourers could spare would not support many exciting stalls. The corporation no longer had financial benefits from the fair, and so did not process in their official capacity. So it was that, while Midsummer Fair, on its pleasant and convenient site close to central Cambridge, turned itself into a fashionable attraction for a broad spectrum of the population, Sturbridge faced ignominious final years. Florence Keynes, mother of John Maynard Keynes, was the mayor of Cambridge at this time, and she officiated at its final year, which she described in her book of reminiscences, *Gathering up the Threads*. 'It was a curious ceremony which had lost all meaning except as a momento of past glories. The first proclamation was made on Barnwell Bridge to the bewilderment of motorists from Newmarket who were held up by the police. The second proclamation took place on the Common in the presence of a couple of women with babies in their arms, and a puzzled youth in charge of an ice-cream barrow bearing the legend "Stop me and Buy one". This was the end'.

9 The villages of Cambridge

Chesterton

With the exception of the area covered by Cambridge castle and royal jurisdiction, and apart from providing diversions for Cambridge students that were forbidden within the bounds the town authorities could control, Chesterton developed like all other farming settlements along the Cam valley until the time when its three open fields were enclosed in 1840. It was after this that the relentless pressures for new housing for Cambridge residents turned much of it into a densely-settled suburb. Later on, the northern part was developed as a sewage works, science park, railway sidings and housing estates but, squeezed in between these, an historic village can still be found.

Part of the Iron Age fort of Arbury is in Chesterton, and the Roman period was particularly important, for much of the walled town lay in this parish, as well as the suburban villas of Arbury, and various cemeteries. The process by which the Roman town and the rural parish that contained it became a royal manor, as it was in 1086, is not understood, but it seems that the appropriation of the defended area by one of the Saxon kings, probably Offa, might have been the significant moment. Taking its place-name (*Cestretone,* or 'farm by the fortified place' in Domesday Book) from the Roman town, a later Saxon village grew up about a mile away from the fortifications, just above the flood-plain of the river. Here, one of the important routeways from Suffolk and east Cambridgeshire, passing through Balsham and Fulbourn, crossed the river by ferry on its way to join the King's Highway, (from Cambridge to the Isle of Ely), at Arbury Camp, and the church and manor house were built near this road. Later there was an early change in the direction of the village's main street, switching from a line that crosses the river to one that runs parallel to it.

The original settlement around the church and manor house filled a small oval area which still contained numerous irregular plots in the nineteenth century (**67**). Slight traces of a former village green on the opposite side were visible in 1987, though this is now just an asphalted verge. At some time during the population expansion of the Norman period a much larger area was developed in an east-westerly direction, following a high street first mentioned in the late thirteenth century. The curving crofts behind the houses on the Enclosure map suggest that these were laid out over already-existing open fields. The crofts run to a parallel back lane (now Scotland Road, but still just 'Back Lane' in 1840) to the north, and a medieval moat, now infilled, may have been the site of a manor house which oversaw this planned expansion. A short parallel road to the south, Water Street, perhaps belongs to a later development on what had previously been

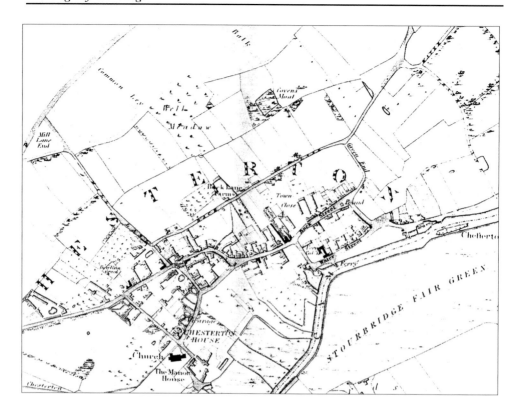

67   *Chesterton in 1830, from a map made by Richard Baker.*

common land or green, a response to the commerce at Sturbridge Fair on the opposite banks of the river. The earliest building here is the Green Dragon, built in the sixteenth century but probably serving traders at the fair from much earlier times. Edward Ward's pamphlet about Sturbridge Fair, published in 1700, mentions 'the Black Bull, where the Country Chapmen generally lodge that come to the Fair, for the sake of rare strong humming Ale, for which 'tis famous; over which they get Drunk, Quarrel, and make Bargains'. Sites of a pound and triangular green are shown on Baker's map of 1830 and could be distinguished by the Chesterton Local History Society in 1987, though today there is only a wide grass verge.

Important medieval routeways through the village were those which led down Ferry Lane to Sturbridge and Newmarket Road, the crossing over to Barnwell Priory, and a path further down the river to Jesus College. This latter path, now ending in Ferry Path and a footbridge over the river to the sixteenth-century Fort St George pub, was the quickest way into Cambridge. In 1668 it was used by Samuel Pepys, who records his pleasure at seeing 'our old walk' at Chesterton and the church where he used to come as an undergraduate. He made a circular walk by coming back on the ferry to Barnwell Priory, 'and so by Jesus College to the town'. The southerly routes all used the footpath that still runs through the churchyard. Only in the nineteenth century did Chesterton Road meet the Cambridge — Ely turnpike road at the extraordinarily awkward junction known as Mitcham's Corner. For foot traffic, the Ferry Path route remained the most popular way to Cambridge until Victoria Bridge was opened in 1890.

To the south of the High Street several lanes ran down to the river, emphasising the importance of river traffic and trade. In some places, such as Water Lane and Ferry Lane, there were clusters of tiny properties down to the river, reflecting the living that could be made there by families too poor to hold more than a negligible piece of land. During the middle ages several ferries already existed to cross the river from the lanes, and control of them was one of the many subjects of dispute between Barnwell Priory, who were the lord of the manor, and the town. These ferries, the last of which were operating until the 1930s, provided far more crossing-places than are now available. In 1900, for example, there were still ten in operation, in addition to those provided by the colleges for their own students who rowed here, despite the bridges then in existence.

Chesterton remained a royal manor until about 1200, after which it was effectively rented out to Barnwell Priory until the dissolution of the monasteries in 1540. It was then bought by Thomas Brakyn, mayor and MP for Cambridge, and he and his successors split parts of the estate by selling long leases on parcels of farmland. Eventually, in the early twentieth century, a large area that was Manor Farm, around King's Hedges, was sold to the County Council, and has subsequently been used for housing estates, schools and, following a sale to Trinity College, part of a science park. The manor house itself, just north-west of the church on the site now used for sheltered bungalows, was rebuilt in the seventeenth century, refaced in the nineteenth century and demolished in 1971.

Some of the parcels of land that were let from the main estate became small manors in their own right or in conjunction with holdings in nearby parishes. The largest and most interesting of these was Wraggs, originally built up by village yeomen. In the late sixteenth century this manor was bought by Thomas Hobson, the Cambridge carrier. It was probably he or his son who built Chesterton Hall in the early seventeenth century. Later in that century the estate passed by marriage to the Pepys family. The house was altered and made more ornate in the nineteenth century, and has now been converted into flats. The Rectory was another unusual manor. In 1227 it was given by Henry III to an abbey at Vercelli in thanks for a cardinal's help in preventing one of the periodic outbursts of civil war, and for much of the middle ages the rectors were Italians, sent from the home abbey. Their residence was Chesterton Tower, an imposing mid-fourteenth century building standing near the church, which has now been restored and is used as offices (**68**). In 1440 the pope agreed to transfer the church and its rectory to King's Hall, later part of Trinity College. The extensive grounds of all three manors, now mostly filled with flats or used for the recreation ground, prevented development of the village in this area and so encouraged growth further to the north.

The church itself was built on a handsome scale, mainly in the fourteenth century but with some thirteenth-century surviving portions and fifteenth-century additions. From the mid nineteenth century it attracted the attention of the Camden Society, who oversaw fairly drastic restoration. The present spire, for example, dates only to 1847. It has an impressive interior, with a rather faded Doom painting and medieval bench ends in the forms of poppy heads and two men dressed in the clothes of about 1430–40, but its best

68   *Chesterton Towers, built in the fourteenth century for priests from Vercelli, in 1875*

feature is its huge country churchyard, filled with important and decorative memorials of various dates. These include three medieval coffin lids which were laid on top of the churchyard wall when William Cole visited in 1769, after having been displaced during the Reformation. There is a good collection of eighteenth-century grave stones, and magnificent nineteenth-century memorials. Perhaps the most touching is the stone commemorating the daughter of an African ex-slave (**69**). Her father had belonged to the Ibo tribe of Nigeria, and after capture and life as a slave, was set free and later worked with the European Anti-Slavery movement, publishing his best-selling memoirs for them. Both he and his English wife died before this child, and it is not known who erected the memorial for her.

The river at Chesterton was important for commercial uses including boat-building up to the late nineteenth century and is still renowned for rowing practice and races and for the boathouses along its banks. Proximity to Cambridge made it attractive to students for other recreational activities. We know they went there to play football in 1581, when the townsmen 'did bring oute there staves wherewith they did so beat the schollers that divers had there heads broken'. Bull and bear-baiting and plays were all forbidden (apparently with little effect) in that century. 'Finding the beare at stake where he had been bayted in the sermon time' was one unsurprised complaint. Later on the university authorities did gain control over public houses, and were able to restrict their number

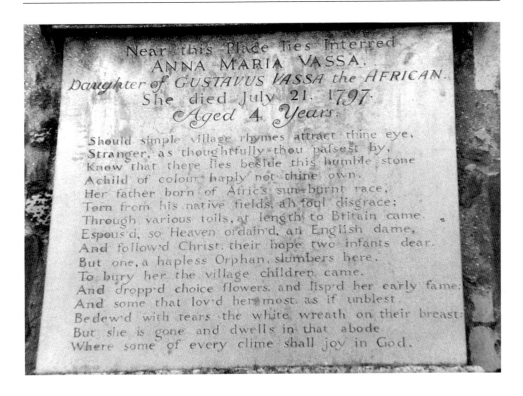

Near this Place lies interred
ANNA MARIA VASSA,
Daughter of GUSTAVUS VASSA the AFRICAN.
She died July 21. 1797.
Aged 4 Years.

Should simple village rhymes attract thine eye,
Stranger, as thoughtfully thou passest by,
Know that there lies beside this humble stone
A child of colour haply not thine own.
Her father born of Afric's sun-burnt race,
Torn from his native fields, ah foul disgrace:
Through various toils, at length to Britain came.
Espous'd, so Heaven ordain'd, an English dame,
And follow'd Christ; their hope two infants dear.
But one, a hapless Orphan, slumbers here.
To bury her the village children came.
And dropp'd choice flowers, and lisp'd her early fame;
And some that lov'd her most, as if unblest,
Bedew'd with tears the white wreath on their breast;
But she is gone and dwells in that abode
Where some of every clime shall joy in God.

69   *A memorial to an African child who died in Chesterton in 1797*

until they lost this power in 1856. Other amusements available that must have brought a variety of university members across the river included bowls, skittles, billiards and the increasingly popular sport of rowing.

The population of Chesterton was first recorded in 1086 when there were 24 peasant families, perhaps about a hundred people, making a living by farming. By 1279 this population had grown hugely, to about 165 taxpayers, probably reflecting a total population of over 800 people. As was usually the case, this figure fell during the years of plague and other problems in the fourteenth century, and recovery was slow, but there was still a good-sized settlement of about 70 households in the sixteenth century, and this gradually doubled, so that when the first census returns were made in 1801 there were 741 inhabitants counted in 150 houses. In the mid nineteenth century Chesterton could still be described as 'large, handsome and pleasantly situated on the north bank of the river Cam'. Speculative builders had already started buying land before an Enclosure Act was granted, and on their holdings dramatic changes were soon underway, though the large areas owned by the Wraggs and the Bensons were not built on until close to the end of the nineteenth century. Land-owning colleges were able to insist on a broad tree-lined road with space left for a walk along the river and large and respectable houses set well back along the Cambridge end of Chesterton Road. When Victoria Bridge was built some land was opened up for upper middle class families, but most areas were packed with terraced

70   *Chesterton in 1838, just before Enclosure, seen from Castle Hill. Note agricultural land and brick pits on the foreground, St Andrew's church at Chesterton in the background, and the lack of a road to the village*

houses for working-class families, huge numbers of whom were college servants, as they still were in living memory. This applied particularly in New Chesterton, the area where royal authorities of the castle and the parish had for so long disputed grazing rights and construction of the occasional ramshackle cottage amidst the middens and brick-pits. An engraving made in 1838 (**70**) shows this rural area just before Enclosure. Housing development was quite slow to start, but after another half century there were several thousand people dwelling here. The first modern cemetery of Cambridge was in use at Histon Road, churches (notably St Luke's, **colour plate 23**) were provided, quarries were infilled (one large brick-pit becoming the recreational Alexandra Gardens), and shops and industrial sites were mingled in residential streets. French's Mill, a mid nineteenth-century brick smock-mill, now partly restored but no longer working, is one relic of times when town and country worked closely together. By 1901 the population approached 10,000. At the end of the twentieth century it is nearly 30,000, and only the ancient centre retains its historic character. Much of the area is now gentrified, with the closing of a brush factory and car repair workshop in the triangle of development next to the castle in the late 1990s perhaps marking the end of one era.

Trumpington

About two miles to the south of Cambridge lies the village of Trumpington, sufficiently far away to still be a rural settlement, only linked to the town by a single interrupted line of well-screened houses set a discreet distance back from the highway. Land here was described as 'of a black moory nature ... subject to frequent overflowings from the river' by the agricultural writer Vancouver, in the eighteenth century. The village is linked to its neighbour Grantchester by a crossing-place of the river, already in use in prehistoric times, and to Cambridge by the river (navigable by shallow craft) and by a road which has been shifted over to its present easterly alignment but which retains the functions of the Roman and medieval through-route.

In 1086 there were 37 households, about 185 people, and this population grew to some hundred landholders in 1279. The population fell after this peak, and there were still less than half this number in the sixteenth century. Despite steady growth in the next four hundred years, it was not until the first census was made in 1801 that there were again a hundred families, 494 people, in the village. Lack of a railway station and the distance to Cambridge, plus restraints on housing for humbler incomers by powerful local squires, limited growth in the period of potential expansion before the usual early twentieth century decline, and after that planning controls were used to protect this attractive village.

The main road that runs through it, a turnpike from 1793–1872, has been moved to the east of its original route. Before this, the London — Royston — Cambridge road ran through the village centre, just west of the church. There it crossed a long-distance route, in use in Roman and probably prehistoric times, running westwards to Grantchester, then on to Bourn and to Ermine Street, and eastwards to Fulbourn and the Icknield Way. The ford over the river served travellers until 1790, when Brasley Bridge was first built. An alternative road to London, through Great Shelford and Saffron Walden, joined the road in Trumpington, and it is also likely that other east-west tracks crossed the parish. One of these must have followed the line taken by the owners of Trumpington Hall for the tree-lined avenue from the main road, for when foundations were being dug for the Eric Gill War Memorial that stands where these two routes meet, the stone base of a medieval wayside cross was found. It can now be seen in the churchyard. Another route to the north of Trumpington Hall leads from an ancient part of Grantchester, where excavations have shown there was settlement in early Anglo-Saxon times. A mound, possibly a Roman barrow but lost without record, was close to where this route crossed the Roman road into Cambridge, and the Green Man pub, once a fifteenth-century open hall, is also significantly nearby.

There were four manors here at the time of Domesday Book, of which two were to have a lasting impact on the village. Trumpington manor was held by the family of the same name from the twelfth to the sixteenth century, and they were resident here until the late fourteenth century. One lord temporarily lost his lands for rebellion against King John. Another had his estate raided by warring barons in 1264, perhaps during his absence, for he was a crusader knight, though probably not the Roger de Trumpington who is commemorated by a magnificent brass in Trumpington church, one of the oldest in Britain (**71**). The estate was sold to the Pychards and then to the Sir Francis Pemberton, Lord Chief Justice of England, whose family still own much of the parish. The Hall is probably on the site of a manor house recorded in the thirteenth century. It was itself first built in about 1600, was thoroughly reconstructed in the eighteenth, and partially turned into flats in the twentieth century. It only had a modest garden up to about 1800, together with an avenue to the main road which followed an older track, but after this a landscaped parkland setting was created. This enclosed the old site of the Camping Close, once used for a medieval form of football, and most of the northern side of the village, and the

71   *The brass of Sir Roger de Trumpington*

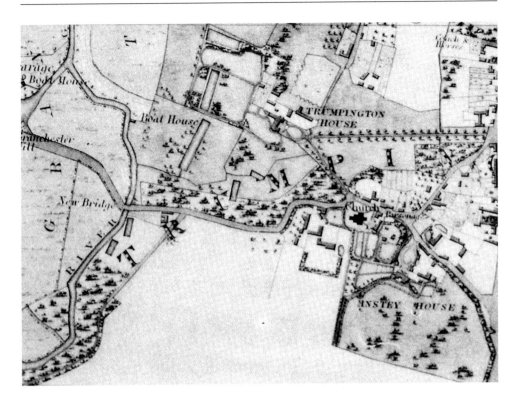

72   *Trumpington in 1830, from a map made by Richard Baker*

triangular village green that is shown on Baker's map of 1830 (**72**). Emparkment and Enclosure also involved the eventual clearance during the nineteenth century of a hamlet known as Dagling End, lying on the old north-south route to the north of the Hall. Much of the mature tree cover around Trumpington, lining the roads and screening houses, is due to the landscaping of Trumpington and Anstey Halls.

Another pre-Conquest manor passed to the Anstey family in the eighteenth century. The manor house stood near the church in 1279. It was rebuilt in the seventeenth century, and at the same time a large garden was laid out, using much of the southerly side of the village around the church. The village was therefore squeezed into development along the road leading out of the old settlement towards the turnpike road. In the nineteenth century the Fosters, a leading Cambridge banking family, bought the estate, extended the house and added many outbuildings. In the mid nineteenth century (when the village as a whole was 'remarkably clean and pleasant') this house was described as 'another fine, spacious mansion', but by the time it was requisitioned by the Government in 1941 much of it was derelict. Later on, the Hall, its outbuildings and its land were used by the Plant Breeding Institute, and their lodge by the Royal Commission on Historical Monuments.

A manor that was sold in the sixteenth century to the Pychards of Trumpington manor was originally given to Ely Abbey by Brihtnoth, hero of the Battle of Maldon, though it was later seized by a Norman lord. It was held locally by the de Cailly family, and it was they who owned the watermill that once stood above Byron's Pool. This is mentioned in Domesday Book and features in Chaucer's *The Reeve's Tale,* where the grinding of corn for a Cambridge college is described. Chaucer's wife was a friend of Lady Blanche de Trumpington, and he may well have known this site.

Cherry Hinton

Cherry Hinton also survived as an attractive village well into the twentieth century (**73**), but the need for housing in recent years has meant that is becoming absorbed into Cambridge almost as much as Chesterton. Its subsoil is chalk, which was extensively quarried and burnt as lime. In the thirteenth century Corpus Christi had its own quarry here, as did King's Hall from the mid fifteenth century. Trinity gatehouse, parts of Peterhouse and Corpus Christi chapel all use Cherry Hinton stone, and stone masons were employed until the late nineteenth century. Cement works were established by 1895, next to a branch railway, and it was their activities which account for the destruction of War Ditches. They were closed in 1984.

The parish of Cherry Hinton once contained the extremes of high chalk downland and low boggy marshes and streams (**colour plate 24**). It is the only area in Cambridge with anything like real hills, for although the village itself is mostly about 15m above sea level the downs to the south rise up to 50m. Within the village there is an area of lower ground which separated the two halves of the settlement until it was drained in the nineteenth century. Before this it was appreciated as good walking and wild-fowling country for dons and students. Henry Gunning, in his *Reminiscences,* says that 'if you started from the other corner of Parker's Piece, you came to Cherry Hinton fen ... In taking this beat, you met with great varieties of wild-fowl, bitterns, plovers of every description, ruffs and reeves, and not infrequently pheasants ... you scarcely ever saw the gamekeeper'. Around the springs that feed Cherry Hinton brook there is still a large pond and marshy area which was referred to by Vancouver as 'an absolute morass'.

The medieval village was built around two centres and manors, Uphall and Nether Hall. Uphall, later known as Church End, had a manor house near the church, sited near a cross-road on the route to Barnwell which probably became more significant as Sturbridge Fair grew. The footpath to Cambridge that is now Mill Road was a popular stroll for academics. In 1406 the owner of the manor, Sir Henry Fitzhugh, granted it to a Swedish religious order, the Brigettines, provided they establish a house there. He eventually left it to the king, to be given to the Brigettines at Syon. After the dissolution of the monasteries it became Crown land. The present house, known as Uphall, was originally a sixteenth-century timber-framed house that was later encased in brick and much altered in the nineteenth century.

The other village centre was around the manor of Nether Hall, on one of the old roads to Cambridge, at the northern end of Mill End Road. This became the larger settlement, and in 1806 consisted of the present High Street and the loop of Mill End Road with the green, village pond, springs, and a wide expanse of water where the roads met. Houses on either side of the High Street are backed by long thin strips, evidently taken in from ploughed open fields during the middle ages, additions to the original Saxon settlements. The manor of Netherhall, like Uphall, belonged to Edith the Fair, Harold's mistress,

73   Cottages in the rural backwater of Cherry Hinton Church End in the early twentieth century

before the Norman Conquest. Later overlords included the dukes of Norfolk and Ann, wife of Richard III. Edward VI gave the manor to St Thomas' Hospital, London, in the sixteenth century. The local manor house probably stood within the present grounds of Cherry Hinton Hall, where a moated site has recently been recognised.

The Rectory at Cherry Hinton also counted as a manor. It was sold to Ely before 1286, and in the fourteenth century was given to Peterhouse. There was one other small manor, Mallet's, recorded from the thirteenth century, roughly opposite the church according to the Enclosure Award. By the mid eighteenth century it belonged to the Serocold family, lords of Uphall, and remained part of that estate. After Enclosure the most important highway was a new road from Fulbourn to the Cambridge road, and the settlement expanded to the south, especially as the chalk quarries became major employers. Cherry Hinton then took on the appearance of a linear village, with a church isolated at one end.

Another change to come over the village started in 1831 when John Okes, a surgeon at Addenbrookes Hospital, bought a large area of land south of the village and built Cherry Hinton Hall. Around it, he made a park out of land that had been closes, orchard, open fields, a barn, and a moated homestead. He struck a particularly good bargain when the Town Water Works Company used the springs at Cherry Hinton to supply Cambridge with drinking water, for he was able to specify that a certain quantity of water be channelled to feed a new weir and ornamental fishponds that he constructed in his park. Cambridge City Council purchased the hall and park and it is now home to the Cambridge Folk Festival and many other events.

10 The later town

Historical outline

At the end of the fifteenth century the fortunes of Cambridge were improving once more. Wastelands are still recorded, but with construction of new colleges capital flowed into the town, providing work for craftsmen and labourers. In 1544 Cambridge was described as 'wele inhabyted and replenysshed with people.' Later in the century there are even complaints about too much subdivision of properties, 'unholsome cottages' being built on 'every lane and corner', and general overcrowding, in contrast to the complaints about derelict plots and empty tenements of earlier years. Maps made later in the sixteenth century show virtually all street frontages lined with properties (**74**) but, however unsavoury the town, at least it contained many gardens, orchards and open spaces, and was so small that no one can have been much more than five minutes stroll from farmland or commons.

This century saw some of the worst enmity between the town and university, and social pressures increased with the departure of the monks and friars and the destruction of buildings that had been expected to last for ever. Shifts in religious persuasions affected the lives of those who could make a fortune or a successful academic career by belonging to the right trend at the right moment, or could be burnt at the stake if they got it wrong. The Counter Reformation under Mary I included royal visitations and compulsory exhibitions of loyalty to the Catholic faith. Bodies of two Protestants were exhumed and burnt in the market place together with many books that were seen as heretical. Cambridge men, Cranmer, Ridley and Latimer, were burnt in Oxford under Mary, and on Jesus Green John Hullier, the vicar of Babraham, was burnt, dynamite from a friendly local bookseller being given to speed his passing.

Ket's Rebellion in the mid sixteenth century was principally a fight between those seeking to enclose more land and holders of common rights. It started in Norfolk, and in Cambridge pride was taken in the way fences were pulled up and thrown into the river. 'Swymming ever more awaye, / Saylinge towarde the castell, / ... Sothe, syr, down to Chesterton / Great store of stakes be gone', was part of one contemporary poem. Some ring-leaders of this rebellion were hanged, but most were pardoned, and their principles, protecting common meadows from enclosure, later meant that most of the greens encircling Cambridge were protected thenceforth.

Growth and prosperity came to a temporary halt with the Civil War in the seventeenth century. Oliver Cromwell was a local man whose support was strong in East Anglia, and he had recently been elected MP for Cambridge. The town generally welcomed the

74   *An extract from John Hamond's map of 1592, showing densely packed houses and churches in the centre, buildings in the market place and the built-up northern frontage of* High Strete *(King's Parade)*

presence of his castle and soldiers, even if they complained about unpaid bills, but the university was in the main Royalist and relationships were strained, though Cromwell in fact ensured that the colleges were treated well. Apart from Cromwell's refortification of the castle, the town was defended by pulling down all bridges except for Great Bridge and the Small Bridges, there was a gun emplacement on Great Bridge, and the town was defended on the south and east with earthen banks and gun emplacements. There was a fort at Four Lamps at the end of Jesus Lane, defensive earthen banks ran through Jesus Green, Parker's Piece, Christ's Pieces and along Lensfield Road, and there were outworks at Chesterton. At one time there were 14,000 Parliamentary troops in Cambridge, many of them quartered in college buildings, and Cambridge was the administrative centre for the New Model Army in East Anglia. King's chapel was used for a drill hall and St John's Old Court for a prison. Some religious images in college chapels were broken, but otherwise the university was not very much affected. For once the town and not the university enjoyed political favour. This situation lasted until the restoration of Charles II, when the privileges of the university were promptly granted again. At this time the Corporation Act came into force, with further royal interference in 1687, making changes to the town's ruling oligarchy though this seems to have had little effect on the pattern of burgesses, mostly from county families from outside the town. They continued to form the corporation, voting for MPs, running the town's affairs in an indolent but reasonably conscientious fashion, and enjoying monumental feasts.

Further decline in the public life of Cambridge is blamed on John Mortlock who, with two of his sons, ran Cambridge from 1788–1835. Mortlock had inherited money from land and the drapery business. He then founded the first bank in Cambridge, so that most of the tradesmen were soon in his debt. In his time, charities lapsed, town property was given for token rents to friends or other corporation members on 99 year leases, and basic matters such as repair of bridges and policing were neglected or left to the university. The income of the borough both from the land it owned and the many bequests left for the benefit of the poor and to provide social or hygiene amenities was diverted to feasting by the burgesses on a prodigious scale, to legal battles, and to the Mortlock family and bank. Mortlock's excuse for his behaviour was that 'without influence, which you call corruption, men will not be induced to support government'. In 1833 a leading article in the Times devoted to Cambridge included the damning results of a Royal Commission. 'Probably no judicial investigation into a private trust ever brought to light more shameless profligacy or more inveterate dishonesty, more bare-faced venality in politics, a more heartless disregard of the claims of the poor, in the perversion of the funds left for their benefit, or a more degrading subserviency to the views of the rich ... or a more entire neglect of their functions and duties as magistrates, than are presented by the evidence now before us'. In 1835 the Municipal Reform Act set up a new corporation, to which none of the old members were elected.

Trade

The river, according to an address made to James I, 'with navigation to the sea, is the life of trafficke to this Towne and Countie'. The medieval trade in corn and fish was still significant, and from the sixteenth century coal from northern England was a valuable import. Wine, with its ready market with the colleges and the burgesses, was always an important item of trade from Europe, and rural supplies of fish, wild-fowl and sedge from the Fens, cheese and butter from the Fen edge villages, and sheep and arable crops from villages to the south became still more abundant as communications by road improved. An important character who made his fortune in the later sixteenth century was Thomas Hobson. One of the first to take advantage of better transport systems, he was a carrier who sent regular deliveries to London by cart and he also hired out horses, a profitable business as most students needed these for transport. Horses were only hired in strict rotation, the origin of the phrase 'Hobson's Choice'. He lived to be 86, and is supposed to have then died out of boredom as his business had to be suspended because an outbreak of plague stopped travel to London. He was a generous benefactor to the town, supporting, for example, the Conduit that brought fresh water to the town.

Changes came with the opening of toll-roads after 1633 and the first stage-coach to London in 1655, followed by others to towns in the midlands and East Anglia. High quality foodstuffs such as butter, fish and wild fowl could now be taken to the expanding London market, though the roads were still bad and had the danger of highwaymen. Samuel Pepys normally took two days for this journey and went on horseback, though it

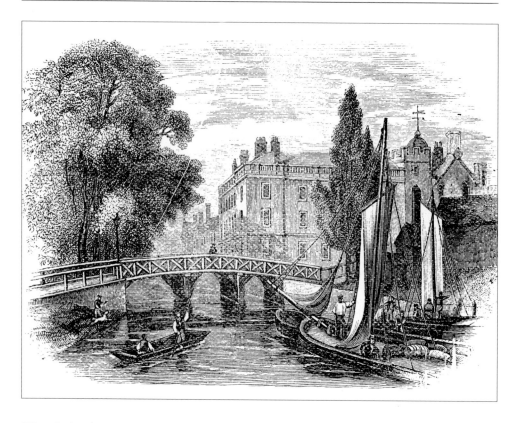

75   *Sailing barges near Queens' College in 1839*

was possible to do it in a fifteen hour day. The eighteenth-century growth in road traffic lead to coaching inns, where coaches could drive in one side, wait while the passengers dined and horses were fed and perhaps changed, and then drive out the other side. The Eagle, though it has lost its back entrance, is still a good example of this kind of inn which was common in Cambridge until the late twentieth century.

After fenland drainage in the seventeenth century, the tidal waters that had flowed to Waterbeach and permitted sea-going vessels to Cambridge stopped at Denver Sluice, so goods had to be unloaded onto barges (**75** and **colour plate 26**). Early in the nineteenth century the river became more silted up, and had to be restricted to boats less than 2 foot 8 inches. The river was dredged and locks rebuilt, but work done was only minimal, and bridges were not replaced. It was fortunate that too much money was not expended at this time, for the arrival of the railway destroyed most of the commercial activity that had revolved around Mill Pool for nearly a thousand years, despite the introduction of steam tugs. Even so, use of waterways to transport certain heavy goods to and from Cambridge continued until the 1930s, and Quayside by Magdalene Bridge, and Newnham were busy well into the twentieth century. Gas water, a by-product of the Cheddars Lane gas-works, and vinegar from the factory that is now part of Magdalene College, were sent out, and coal was the main import.

76   The market place before the fire of 1849

The medieval market cross remained the heart of the town, where proclamations were read and commercial life was centred. The old market place was the centre for everyday commercial exchange for the people of Cambridge and the surrounding villages, as well as serving the needs of a wider region for foreign goods (**76**). In 1613 the site was paved, and in the following year the fountain head for Hobson's Conduit was a glamorous as well as a useful addition. These changes made appreciable differences, and John Evelyn's Diary for 1654 records 'The market place is very ample, and remarkable for old Hobson the pleasant carriers beneficence of a fountain'. The medieval tradition of separate areas for various products was maintained, with a garden market around the cross and fountain, a fish market on Peas Hill, the butchery (the Shambles) between the King's Ditch and town hall, and corn and poultry in the north-east corner. Stalls also stood under the medieval Tollbooth. It was not until a widespread fire in 1849 cleared shops and other buildings behind Great St Mary's that a suitably spacious market place could be laid out. Permanent stores such as Eaden Lilley and Joshua Taylor were being founded at this time too, and Hobson's Conduit was moved to the Lensfield Road/Trumpington Road corner.

Agricultural markets were so important in the nineteenth century that more spacious specialised centres had to be provided. The hay market was moved from a site near St Clement's to Pound Hill in the upper town in 1820, followed by the cattle market, previously held on King Street, in 1843. A corn exchange was set up in Downing Street in

77   *A barn and farmyard behind the Folk Museum, where French prisoners of war are supposed to have been kept during the Napoleonic Wars*

1842, and had its own purpose-made building (now used for concerts and plays) behind the Town Hall in 1875. In 1885 the cattle market moved again, this time to the site on Hills Road which still bears this name though it is used for light industries and the Junction, a centre for pop concerts and discos.

The White Horse Inn and the farm that preceded it served as a victualling stop for drovers bringing stock into Cambridge even before it properly became an inn in the early eighteenth century. Carts would be taken through the wide double doors, horses and cattle would be fed and watered in the farmyard beyond, and drovers with a long distance to cover could find lodging. Within the rooms of the Folk Museum can still be seen the cupboards under fold-down sleeping benches where men slept with their days takings safe beneath them. Land behind the Folk Museum and Kettles Yard was still a farm supplying milk for a daily milk-round in the mid twentieth century. Its old thatched barn was said to have lodged French prisoners of war during the Napoleonic Wars **(77)**.

Industry

According to the poll tax returns of 1512 the population of Cambridge included brewers, freemasons (ie skilled workman), shoemakers and tailors. In 1561 there is mention of a kiln near the hermitage of St Anne at Trumpington Gate, and of a 'beerebruehouse at the greate brydge by the Ryver side'. Another licence was sold 'to set a pump in the King's streame and from the same to convey water under the ground to his bruehouse', despite the other well-known uses of the river and King's Ditch. Harleston Lane, named after the manor house and farm of Roger de Harleston, mayor in 1356, became Thompson's Lane in the sixteenth century, after the Thompson family which had a brewery by the river here, about 1520–1750.

Printing, supported by the university whose members were its main clients, was to become one of Cambridge's few long-lived industrial successes, and it too began in Cambridge in this century. In 1521 the first printing press was set up, with Erasmus as one of its early authors. Religious controversies at this time made life difficult for printers, as many works were liable to be condemned by one side or another, but they also made for a lively market, especially when books were publicly burnt. It was in this century that the university secured an invaluable right to licence the printing of any work of which it approved. The Cambridge University Press, officially established by Henry VIII in 1534, originated with this privilege. In the sixteenth century most of those involved with printing and selling books were foreigners, mainly German. Well-known names from the early days of Cambridge printing are Thomas Buck in the early seventeenth century, John Bowtell, who made a fortune through printing and innovative book-binding, and his nephew of the same name. In the late seventeenth century the University Press became an official part of the university, with its own printing press, to be replaced with the Pitt Press in 1804. Only booksellers at the fairs were not controlled by the university, one reason why the auctions at Sturbridge Fair were so popular. There was a paper mill on Newmarket Road to supply this trade by the late sixteenth century.

Otherwise, evidence for industries in Cambridge is slight, just as it had been in earlier times. The medieval cloth industry continued at a low level until the eighteenth century, when there were complaints about the damage done to the town by competition from India. After this the development of industrial centres in the North and midlands must have finished manufacture on any scale, though the Spinning House used the cheap compulsory labour of the inmates of the House of Correction until 1800, and tenter yards, where cloth was stretched, existed on the old Botanic Garden site and on Castle Hill, evidence of some continued production. There were saltpetre factories in Cambridge and Barnwell in the seventeenth century, and archaeological excavations on Thompson's Lane have revealed an eighteenth-century kiln that was used for firing peg-tiles and flower-pots. This area near Magdalene Bridge continued to be used for commerce and industry (**78**), becoming somewhat derelict before it was converted into smart housing, shops, cafes and a punt-hire centre in the late twentieth century (**colour plate 25**). Boatmen's cottages were cleared for Magdalene's new accommodation south of the bridge in the 1930s, and an electricity power station in Thompson's Lane closed and lost its tower in 1966. Further up the river gas production stopped in 1969, but at the time of writing two of its gasometers are still standing (**colour plate 27**).

78   *Quayside and Thompson's Lane power station, which closed in 1966. See colour plate 25 for the same view today*

In 1845 the railway arrived, though it was strongly opposed by many interests, especially the university, which forced it to be sited well away from the town. There were six different companies running trains into Cambridge, each with its own stock and facilities, and its construction also increased the amount of industrial development in that area. Several coal yards were built behind Station Road and there was cement making and grain milling at Foster's mill. To supply materials for the houses of industrial workers, brick and tile works were developed at Cherry Hinton and on Coldham's Lane using the local clay. There was cement manufacture in Romsey Town using chalk marl which occurred there, and along Newmarket Road there were brick, tile, iron and gas works, and coal yards etc. Local breweries, as usual, accompanied these developing industries. Panton Brewery in Panton Street was later taken over by Greene King and survived until 1969, when it was demolished. Dale's Brewery in Gwydir Street closed in 1955, but still stands, and the last independent brewery, the Star Brewery, was brewing in Newmarket Road until 1972.

A very different type of industrial development began at the end of the nineteenth century. This was the design and manufacture of scientific instruments, initially for university use, leading to the creation of Pye's (now Phillips) in Chesterton, and the Cambridge Instrument Company. These in turn led development in high technology and science-based industries, so that at the end of the twentieth century Cambridge is in the forefront of this field. There are science parks all around the town, and with the arrival of Microsoft from America Cambridge has resigned itself to computer technology rivalling education as a means to earn a livelihood. Many research institutes, often sited outside the town, were also attracted to the area because of university connections in the twentieth century.

Health, public services and welfare

At the very beginning of the sixteenth century Cambridge lost the nunnery of St Radegund and the hospital of St John, the latter in particular probably being a far greater loss to the poor and sick of the town than was acknowledged at the time and by later historians. Barnwell Priory, another modest benefactor of the poor, was dissolved a few years later, and after this there was very little provision made for the needy. Cambridge was generally considered an unhealthy place, and outbreaks of plague continued to afflict the inhabitants until, as in London, the serious attacks of 1665–6 proved to be the last. Pest houses were built on Midsummer Common and later on Coldham's Common, and careful arrangements were made to visit and to provision them. Regulations were made to stop contagion by isolating victims, and members of the university always left town. Sturbridge Fair was cancelled on several occasions, and even the mayor's feasts were abandoned. The poor suffered dreadfully in these times, for no tradesmen would bring food to the town and most of those with money had left. In 1630 things were so bad that the king ordered national collections be made to relieve Cambridge inhabitants, and thousands of pounds were donated in London alone. In the last outbreak deaths were counted and amounted to about 920, approximately one in eight of the population. Records show that plague victims in St Clement's parish were buried on Jesus Green, and it was probably normal to bury near the pest-houses where they died. It was only in the final years of the plague that Cambridge got permission from Parliament to use Coldhams Common for permanent pest houses to isolate its victims. As the need passed these houses were never built, and in 1703 the temporary ones were removed. The lack of permanent provision for the sick was understood, and money for 'a small physical hospital' was left to the town by a local doctor, John Addenbrooke, in 1719, though it was not until 1766 that anything was done. The original building resulting from this benefaction was only the size of a house, and it was replaced in 1865 with Old Addenbrookes Hospital, now restored as the Judge Institute of Management Studies.

We cannot tell how much elementary education was provided for town children by the various religious houses and chantries which abounded in medieval Cambridge, but with their dissolution opportunities virtually disappeared, being mainly restricted to choir boys. At Jesus College a small grammar school was created by Alcock in addition to the college itself, but this, like all the chantry schools, was lost later in the sixteenth century. The loss was deplored, and in 1576 the Town Council were calling for action towards providing a grammar school, though nothing came of this. Then, in 1615, Stephen Perse, a fellow of Gonville and Caius who had made a fortune in medicine, left money for a school to provide free education for a hundred boys. His school stood in Free School Lane until 1890, when the Perse moved to its present site. The funds were badly managed, like most trusts in Cambridge, and in 1703 another scheme was set up to educate poor children, known as the 'Charity Schools.' Five new schools were built, mainly supported by the Church. These had a rather mixed history and some very low standards but at least provided an elementary education for both boys and girls, and the same charity still gives support to Cambridge primary schools.

Cambridge's water supply was from increasingly polluted resources, such as wells sited adjacent to graveyards, the river and King's Ditch. Following an outbreak of plague in 1574 Andrew Perne, master of Peterhouse, proposed that fresh clean water be brought from springs in the chalk at Nine Wells in Great Shelford. Eventually, in 1610, a channel was built from the Vicar's Brook, south of Cambridge, and water was piped to a fountain in the Market Square. Unfortunately, so many supplies were taken from Hobson's Brook before it reached the town, it completely failed in its initial aim of flushing out the King's Ditch, though it did bring some clean water to the townspeople. The Conduit Head itself, built of stone in an ornate renaissance style, complete with scallops, cartouches, putti and royal arms, was moved to the Trumpington Street corner in 1865, and streams still flow along the open gutters, best seen near the Fitzwilliam Museum. One of the loudest supporters of this scheme was the carrier Thomas Hobson, and it was his name that was attached to both Hobson's Brook and Hobson's Conduit.

In the mid nineteenth century, overcrowding led to worsening health problems, most obviously recognised as typhoid outbreaks. This was known to be linked to polluted water supplies, and proposals were made to bring fresh water from another source of chalk springs, this time at Cherry Hinton. A well was sunk and a reservoir and pumping station were constructed on Lime Kiln Hill. Later works in the nineteenth century included another pumping station at Fulbourn, and these two stations supplied Cambridge until 1921, when the Fleam Dyke Works took over. Health scares also led to pressure for a modern sewage system. In 1895 Cheddars Lane Pumping Station was completed, designed to pump into the new sewage farm at Milton. Its brick built engine- and boiler-house, handsome chimney, station engineers cottage and most of the original equipment have been preserved as part of the Cambridge Museum of Technology, and can be seen in action at regular Steaming Weekends.

Law and order

By a charter dating back to the days of Henry III responsibility for policing was held jointly by the town and university, with the university taking the leading role. This in itself led to conflicts, especially in the sixteenth century when the 'unreverent maner' of the mayor was criticised, but an oath acknowledging the university's precedence had to be sworn until 1856. Both authorities shared use of the Tolbooth as a prison after the university's use of the castle became impracticable. The medieval gaol was considered a disgrace, but it was not replaced until the very end of the eighteenth century. When visited by the penal reformer John Howard there was 'a room below for criminals called the Hole, 21 feet by 7, and above a room called the Cage. No Courtyard, no water, no (food) allowance'. Eventually, in 1788, the gaol moved to Downing Place and then Parker's Piece. This was only used until 1878, when the gaol on Castle Hill was used jointly with the county.

In 1628 a joint workhouse and house of correction, later known as the Spinning House, was built, first on Castle Hill and later outside Barnwell Gate, where it stood until 1901. It was replaced by a police and fire station and is now part of the City Council's offices. Wool and flax were supplied to provide employment, and it functioned for nearly the next three centuries as a strange mixture of punishment and social care. Other punishments included continued use of the stocks, pillory and gallows in the market place, and executions for witchcraft on Jesus Green (a woman was hanged here for keeping a tame frog in the sixteenth century). When William Cole was a boy and stayed with his grandmother in a house at the foot of Magdalene Bridge he saw a woman ducked in the river there for scolding. She was let down into the river three times from a chair hung by a pulley to a beam on the timber bridge. The most feared keepers of the law always seem to have been the college proctors, or 'bull-dogs'. One of their powers was the expulsion or arrest of any woman over whom there was a suspicion of prostitution or loose behaviour. This responsibility lasted from 1317 until 1894, and only stopped after furious complaints from the town about imprisonment of entirely innocent girls.

Greens, commons and the Backs

The greens encircling Cambridge which were so fiercely maintained in the sixteenth century were to undergo a few changes in later centuries, though it is the survival of so much of their essential character which is most remarkable.

The first area to change was between the river and the West Fields, land which had provided valuable common grazing land on low-lying meadows. King's and Queens' had obtained land here in the fifteenth century and then, between 1610 and 1613, St John's and Trinity acquired the rest of the pasture known as Long Green, giving the colleges control of the whole area that became the Backs. A cook at Trinity named Edward Parker had somehow obtained a lease on Garret Hostel Green, and when Trinity wanted to build here they were able to exchange this lease with the town for a patch of arable land in the open fields of Barnwell, known to this day as Parker's Piece. In low evening sunlight very slight traces of ridge and furrow can be seen on this invaluable open space, which was ploughed until 1612, then grazed until 1812. From the early seventeenth century therefore, colleges controlled the whole of the riverside meadows from the Great Bridge to Small Bridges.

The river regularly flooded, which deterred most building works, though some, such as Wren's Library at Trinity did go ahead. Loggan's map of 1688 shows this area still pleasantly used for meadows, and although major schemes to create classic new landscapes, like those of the great country houses of the time, were proposed these were largely resisted in the eighteenth century. Nevertheless, the influences of designers such as Capability Brown are apparent in the ways that agriculture, recreation, natural features

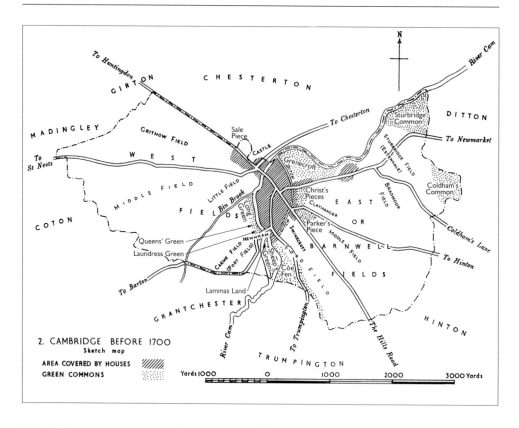

79   *The greens and commons of Cambridge in about 1700*

and the increasingly elegant college buildings were blended together over the next two centuries. King's and Queens' have been content to retain the rural aspect of their greens and, though there is no arable land as there was in the eighteenth century, animals grazing there still add to the beauty and peaceful atmosphere of their famous views (**colour plate 28**). St John's, Trinity and Clare have more formal grounds, with sweeping lawns, sophisticated gardens and walks designed for strolling academics, apparent in many of the views recorded from 1688 onwards.

At the beginning of the nineteenth century Swinecroft and St Thomas' Leys south of the town were taken for Downing College, but when the Enclosure acts came into force nearly all the other green areas had to be maintained, monuments to one of the rare examples of Cambridge people successfully fighting to retain ancient rights. There were even a few additions, as fragments of the open fields such as Christ's Pieces were left behind when developments spread, and this arable land was used first for grazing and then for recreation. Today there are twelve commons in Cambridge, covering about 95 hectares. Grazing on them is now let to farmers, controlled by an officer known as the Pinder. Coldham's, Sturbridge and Midsummer Commons, Sheep's, Laundress and Queens' Greens and Coe Fen are let for cattle, mares and geldings from 1 April to 31 October, but Lammas Land is not currently grazed. Grenecroft is divided by Victoria

Bridge into Jesus Green (a purely recreational area) and Midsummer Common where, in addition to cattle grazing, Midsummer Fair is held and there are other amusements such as circuses, funfairs and a huge annual firework display (**79**).

The town plan and its buildings

During most of this period, as in the middle ages, it would be the town's rural nature that would strike a modern visitor most strongly. To begin with, apart from the arable land and meadows that surrounded it and projected into the inhabited areas, there were wide stretches of marshy open countryside freely available for hunting and shooting. Henry Gunning, recalling the days before Enclosure, writes of his own passion for shooting, shared by a large number of the students. 'In going over the land now occupied by Downing-terrace, you generally got five or six shot at snipe. Crossing the Leys, you entered on Cow Fen, this abounded with snipes. Walking through the osier bed on the Trumpington side of the brook, you frequently met with a pheasant. From thence to the lower end of Pemberton's garden was one continued marsh, which afforded plenty of snipes, and in the month of March a hare or two'. This was the landscape that began a few minutes walk from Cambridge market until 1800.

The late sixteenth-century town included yards behind almost all the street frontages. Houses often had shops or workshops on their ground floors, with minor industrial processes undertaken here or in the backyards. One example of this is a series of ovens excavated on Bridge Street, and another is an ice-house, found under Eaden Lilleys. This was about 7m deep, with a hemispherical brick dome. At this time properties began to be sublet and divided, and tenements were added behind the main properties. In the late sixteenth century a long programme of work began to turn a jumble of lanes and buildings around Great St Mary's and the Old Schools into the wide high street of King's Parade and the elegant buildings and grassed quadrangle that we have today. It was two centuries before this work was complete, and even so grandiose plans to remodel the town in baroque style with a giant piazza in front of King's chapel, were only realised in the university's Senate House, built by Gibb, 1722–30.

One measure of the generally improved prosperity of the town in the sixteenth century is the increase in the number of domestic buildings which are still with us, though many were cleared away in the frenzy of development Cambridge suffered in the 1970s. These include a scatter of two- and three-storey houses with jettied upper floors in the central area, notably in Free School Lane, King's Parade, Peas Hill, Market Hill, Botolph Street and Bene't Street, all of them heavily altered and usually converted into shops. There is still a very attractive row of houses of this date in Little St Mary's Lane and several delightful jettied two-storey blocks along Magdalene Street, Bridge Street and Northampton Street. Early timbers of some of these buildings are exposed, including obscene carvings above No. 25. There is a particularly impressive row of early sixteenth century three-storey houses near Holy Sepulchre, extensively restored and converted to shops in 1977. The Old Vicarage on Thompson's Lane is another interesting building in this area. Public houses of this date include the Fort St George, the Little Rose on Trumpington Street and the Pickerel on Bridge Street. The Folk Museum on Castle Street was originally a sixteenth-century farm building, though unfortunately the Three Tuns, further up the street and infamous as an inn frequented by Dick Turpin, has been pulled down. In the villages, the Red Lion in Cherry Hinton and the Green Dragon in Chesterton are sixteenth-century pubs, and the fifteenth-century Green Man in Trumpington has additions of this date. These pubs, and many others known from this time, were the centres for various dubious social happenings. For example, at the Blue Boar in Trinity Street an Eton boy died in 1577 through 'laughing exceedingly' during cock-fighting, obviously a common sport. There was bear-baiting as well as more innocent pursuits such as bowls at Chesterton, and heretical religious debates at the White Horse fuelled the Reformation. Archaeological discoveries of large amounts of pottery in the town centre probably belong to similar inns. One early seventeenth-century pit-group found under Barclay's bank in Benet Street included sherds of at least 140 mugs, porringers, serving dishes, storage jars, pans, platters and chamber pots.

Visitors from London in the seventeenth century found Cambridge a squalid place, with narrow streets and old-fashioned timber buildings. A paving Act of 1544 made every householder responsible for repairing and paving the street opposite, but rubbish still accumulated faster than it could be moved. From 1544 to 1788 the town and university had joint responsibility for cleanliness, and serious attempts were made, for example, to force butchers to carry away their rotting waste, to stop stable-owners dumping muck in the streets and to prevent pigs wandering at will. Official carters were appointed to collect what was still left, but petitions to have dung hills removed, for example ones on Pound Hill in 1790 'close to our water spring and we have no other to use for eating and drinking', are a regular entry in the town's records. Celia Fiennes in 1647 said that 'the Buildings are old and indifferent the Streets mostly narrow except near the Market place which is pretty spacious', though her descriptions of college grounds are enthusiastic. John Evelyn's Diary for 1654 records 'the whole town is situate in a low dirty unpleasant place, the streets ill-paved, the air thick and infected by the fens, nor are its churches (of which St Mary's is the best) anything considerable, in compare to Oxford'. Apart from being 'abominably dirty', if two wheelbarrows met on even the broadest street it would take half an hour before they could clear themselves, according to Edward Ward in the late seventeenth century, and eighteenth-century commentators were equally appalled. Above all, it was the 'meanness' of Cambridge, that is its appearance of being a large village with a few grand colleges in it, that was remarked upon. When a German scholar Zacharias Conrad von Uffenbach came to use Cambridge libraries in 1710 he complained 'The place itself is not at all large, and about as mean as a village, ... and were it not for the many fine *collegia* here, it would be one of the sorriest places in the world. Nor is the entertainment good; one must dine everyday nearly alike, as on mutton etc'. The colleges were still made of undressed stone or old red bricks at this time, but during the eighteenth century many were faced with ashlar stone and sash-windows replaced the small casements. In 1763 Horace Walpole commented 'The colleges are much cleaned and improved since my days ... but the town is tumbling about their ears'. An act was passed in 1788 for paving, cleaning and lighting the town, but little was done under the Mortlock regime and the general state of the streets continued to horrify its visitors.

In 1747 space in front of the medieval Tolbooth was let to the county for a Shire Hall.

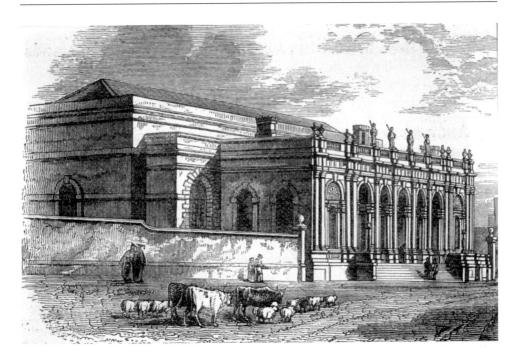

80   An imposing façade of the Victorian Shire Hall on Castle Hill, now demolished

This consisted of two Law Courts above, and an open space beneath which was used for market stalls, as in the Tolbooth. Then, in 1782, the town at last brought itself to replace their old building with a new Town Hall, designed by James Essex, though unfortunately this was obscured by the Shire Hall. When in 1842 the County's lease on its Shire Hall was nearly up, it vacated the site for a new building on Castle Hill (**80**). Their building was converted to form part of the Town Hall, and various nineteenth-century additions to it were made, including a larger Assembly Hall and a public library. As bureaucracy increased this mixture of offices etc was not enough, and in 1932 they were all pulled down, and the present Guildhall erected on the site.

Just under 10,000 people lived in Cambridge in 1800, most of them within the old central area bounded by King's Ditch. Then came the Enclosure acts of 1801 and 1807, and it was possible to open up areas for housing development and eventually to relieve the overcrowding in the centre. Land which had been farmed as strips since late Saxon times was now divided between those who still had rights in the fields, and they could now farm in enclosed fields or sell for housing or any other purpose, although grazing rights on common land were maintained. Partly due to the sell-offs made during Mortlock's era, by which time it was clear how much money would be made by anyone holding even small parcels, the town itself held very little land, and changes were slow to come, as so much land in open fields belonged to the university, colleges and the Panton family, heirs of Barnwell Priory. Thomas Panton died just before an award was made to him, and his executors had to sell quickly, a situation which led to early and very rapid growth in

Barnwell, where the population grew in the nineteenth century from 250 to nearly 28,000. Development, especially after 1850, was so overcrowded it rapidly became a notorious area of slums, and parts were later cleared and replaced. Another part of this estate became New Town, stretching south from Lensfield Road, centred on Panton Street. Colleges tended to hold onto land and then use it for more expensive housing. Their main contribution to early nineteenth-century building was along main roads such as Maids Causeway, Lensfield Road and Trumpington Road, where they built high quality housing with large plots of land behind. The pattern of settlement achieved is shown on Moule's map, published in 1837 (**colour plate 29**).

Within the old town in the mid nineteenth century things had changed surprisingly little. Nearly everyone still lived within a mile of the centre, all too many of them in crowded tenements piled up behind the street frontages, without drainage or running water, and generally in a worse condition than their medieval counterparts who had benefited from more spacious accommodation and rights to arable land and grazing for their stock. It was in the second half of this century that building works really got under way for the benefit of the bulk of the population. At one end of town, later nineteenth-century development along Mill Road, an old field track, was for the working classes, many of them railway workers and men employed in the other industries attracted by the new communications. It was generally to a higher standard than the earlier Barnwell slums, and most of it survives. The area was isolated by lack of a railway bridge until 1890, and so was particularly well supplied with shops and other services. Here, too, there were areas owned by colleges who held onto land until better housing was needed, particularly when fellows were able to marry. Gonville and Caius land south of Parker's Piece, for example, has houses different to most of the area. After 1840 land in Chesterton came available for development, and this also followed the pattern of rapid use of land in private ownership, and slower growth of upper middle class housing where colleges had control.

Housing developments in west Cambridge also had a distinctive character. Nearly all land here was held by the university or colleges, who had no need for the money from its sale and who appreciated the rural views that extended from the borders of several colleges. Then, in 1882, college fellows were at last given permission to marry and to live outside their colleges. Large family homes with spacious grounds were built for them on the land their colleges now owned, and extensive playing fields were laid out for the increasing needs of student sports. As most of Cambridge continued to be surrounded with farms and meadows used by dairymen, butchers and graziers, the overall setting of the town was maintained. Charles Bell, a resident of Gloucester Street, off Castle Street, remembered in 1889 the corn fields where he chased partridges and rabbits, round the back of Castle Hill, and also Castle Hill itself, with 'squalid houses on either side, and teaming with dirty children'.

As the population expanded outside the medieval town the Church of England, prompted by the success of Nonconformist missions, was remembering its responsibilities both to its congregations and to the decaying fabric of the buildings it had inherited. The Camden Society began in Cambridge, and was influential here as elsewhere in inspiring restoration work that is to our eyes heavy-handed, but was probably necessary after years of neglect. Holy Sepulchre (or Round Church) was tackled first, in

81   All Saints in the Jewry, once standing opposite St John's College

82   St Andrew the Great, also demolished in the nineteenth century, in a less academic part of the town

the 1830s, being effectively rebuilt. Almost all the medieval churches in the town and the villages were extensively repaired in the later years of the nineteenth century and others were demolished entirely, only the little Leper Chapel escaping lightly. The small basically Saxon structure of St Giles, still serving the impoverished, disreputable and fast-growing community of the upper town, was taken down and a monstrously large building in a high church tradition was put up in 1870. All Saints in the Jewry's tower had a peculiar arch **(81)** through which traffic along Trinity Street had to pass, which was considered too much of an obstruction, so it too was taken down, being replaced with All Saints in Jesus Lane. St Andrew the Great's medieval structure **(82)** was also replaced with a Victorian building, this time on the same site. New churches too, were built where there were new congregations — Christ Church, St Paul's, St Barnabas and St Matthew's in Barnwell, and St Luke's in New Chesterton, for example. Equally fine churches and chapels could now be built by the Nonconformists, such as the magnificent Emmanuel Church and school on Trumpington Street, **(colour plate 31)** in 1874, and at long last (but most magnificently of all) in 1890, the Catholic church on the corner of Lensfield and Hills Road was opened. Gothic architecture was the inspiration for churches of all denominations, and the impression they give is of scaled-up village churches.

By the end of the nineteenth century Cambridge had a population of over 50,000, a university that had modernised itself beyond recognition, and a town that was at last an independent authority and had developed vastly improved public services. It now had proper schools for all its children, a hospital and workhouse, police officers and a new prison, effective water and sewage systems, museums, a theatre, gas and electric lighting, modern offices for both town and county authorities and many new churches. Its atmosphere, though, still had much that was rural about it, both physically and emotionally, more like a group of interlocking villages than a modern urban centre. Its economy was still mostly that of a market town with sophisticated service industries which fitted themselves around the life and buildings of a world-renowned university.

Much of the twentieth century remained on a similar trajectory, but change became faster from the 1970s onwards, despite the Holford Report of 1954's policy that Cambridge should remain a modestly-sized university town and that development should generally not be allowed. The population of both town and university was growing fast, redevelopment fever meant the loss of many old buildings and streets in favour of new shopping centres and offices, and coping with cars became a major unresolved issue. Towards the end of the century there was a somewhat greater range of industries, often linked to the university and research, with science parks a feature of the town's outskirts. Tourism now brings about 3 million visitors to Cambridge a year and education has become broader, with a new university joining the old, and extensive provision for language students and other private institutions. As of old, shopping is a major part of the economy (**colour plate 30**) and so, still, are all the administrative services, with many central and local government offices located here. Greens and commons, some of them still managed as semi-wild areas or brought alive with grazing animals, bringing a rural feel to the heart of the town, and a village feeling rather than a sense of belonging to one great city persists. This is not now based on houses clustered around a parish church as it was in the middle ages, but more on interest-groups, colleges, professions and neighbourhoods. The social and economic needs of the modern city are therefore well served within an historic community, based as it is so firmly on ancient structures.

Further reading

There are a very great number of books about Cambridge, but nearly all are principally or entirely concerned with the university. Of these, the most readable for descriptions of buildings and also the best illustrated, is Tim Rawle's *Cambridge Architecture,* (1985, reprinted 1993). For life within the university, Elisabeth Leedham-Green's *A Concise history of the University of Cambridge* (1996) is a superb account. For twentieth-century history *Images of Cambridge* by Michael Petty (1994) and *Britain in Old Photographs: Cambridge* (1996) by Chris Jakes give a lot of information and original photographs. The best historical accounts are probably still those contained within the Victoria County Histories for Cambridge. Volume II (1948) has details of the religious houses, Volume III (1959) medieval and later historical accounts, Volume V (1973) Trumpington and Volume IX (1989) Chesterton.

In-depth architectural descriptions are most authoritatively given in two volumes on Cambridge by the Royal Commission on Historical Monuments (1959), and of great value still are the four massive volumes of *The Architectural History of the University of Cambridge,* by Robert Willis and John Willis Clark (1886, reprinted 1988). Other classic early works that are still valuable reading are Maitland's *Township and Borough* (1898) and Gray's *Dual Origins of the town of Cambridge* (1908). Archaeological accounts of discoveries made for more than a century can be found in the annual volumes of Cambridge Antiquarian Society. There are also now many independently published archaeological excavation reports, mainly by Cambridge Archaeology Unit.

Since the first publication of this book the results of many years' excavation have been published as *Roman Cambridge: Excavations on Castle Hill 1956-1988*, John Alexander and Joyce Pullinger 2000, Proceedings of Cambridge Antiquarian Society 88.

Atkinson, T. D. and Clark, J. W. (1897), *Cambridge described and illustrated,* Macmillans

Browne D. M. (1974) 'An Archaeological gazetteer of the city of Cambridge', *Proceedings of Cambridge Antiquarian Society 65.*

Cam H. M. (1933) 'The origin of the borough of Cambridge: a consideration of Prof. Carl Stephenson's theories', *Proceedings of Cambridge Antiquarian Society* 35, 3–53.

Clark, J. W. and Gray, A. (1921), *Old plans of Cambridge,* Heffers

Coppock, H. C. (1984) *Over the Hills to Cherry Hinton* (private)

Gray, A. (1908) *The dual origins of the town of Cambridge,* Cambridge Antiquarian Society

Gray, A. (1925) *The Town of Cambridge: a history,* Heffers

Hall, C. P, and Ravensdale, J. (1976)*The West Fields of Cambridge,* Cambridge Antiquarian Record Society.

Haslam, J. (1984) 'The development and topography of Saxon Cambridge', *Proceedings of Cambridge Antiquarian Society 72,* 113–29

Leedham-Green, E. (1996) *A concise history of the University of Cambridge,* Cambridge University Press

Liversidge, J. (1977) 'Roman burials in the Cambridge area', *Proceedings of Cambridge Antiquarian Society 67,* 11–38

Maitland, F. W. (1898) *Township and borough,* Cambridge University Press

Palmer, W. M (1928, reprinted 1976) *Cambridge Castle* Oleander Press

Petty, M. (1994) *Images of Cambridge* Breedon Books

Rawle, T. (1985) *Cambridge architecture* Andre Deutsch

Steegman, J. (1940) *Cambridge,* Batsford

RCHM (1959) *City of Cambridge* HMSO

VCH, Cambridge and the Isle of Ely, Institute of Historical Research, London

Willis, R. and Clark, J. W. (1886, reprinted 1988), *The architectural history of the university of Cambridge and of the colleges of Cambridge and Eton,* Cambridge University Press

Index

If you are interested in purchasing
other books published by Tempus, or in case you have
difficulty finding any Tempus books in your local bookshop,
you can also place orders directly through our website

www.tempus-publishing.com

or from

BOOKPOST
Freepost, PO Box 29,
Douglas, Isle of Man
IM99 1BQ
Tel 01624 836000
email bookshop@enterprise.net